Pathways to Adolescent Male Violent Offending

This book differentiates between categories of adolescent male offending and explores the behavioral and social profiles of those who become involved in violent offending and organized crime.

Using self-reported and arrest data, the book examines the key stages of male adolescent offending with a view to early recognition of behaviors that leave young men vulnerable to criminal exploitation and the escalation of violence. It also explains the importance of understanding crime motivations, how young men view themselves when they offend, and the emotions that they experience. Rather than looking at violent offending as a single category of behavior, the book helps readers differentiate between types of adolescent violence and understand the underlying psychological and social causes. It offers an insight into the journey of young people who are criminally exploited and those who become involved in committing acts of serious violence and organized crime. It does so by using data from official records, self-reported offending, and the narratives of young people. Each chapter focuses on a particular stage of offending with a view to early identification, support, and diversion.

Pathways to Adolescent Male Violent Offending is aimed at practitioners in youth offending services, youth work, policing, and education. It will also be useful for students of forensic and investigative psychology, criminal justice, policing, and child and adolescent mental health.

Sally-Ann Ashton works as Research Scientist at the Texas Juvenile Crime Prevention Center at Prairie View A&M University, USA. Her PhD from the University of Huddersfield explored the social and psychological risk associated with gang membership and desistance. She has continued to research co-offending, youth gang membership, knife crime, and child criminal exploitation in England with a view to early identification of vulnerable adolescents and diversion from the criminal justice system.

Routledge Studies in Criminal Behaviour

For more information about this series, please visit: https://www.routledge
.com/Routledge-Studies-in-Criminal-Behaviour/book-series/RSCB

Pathways to Adolescent Male Violent Offending

Sally-Ann Ashton

Routledge
Taylor & Francis Group

LONDON AND NEW YORK

First published 2023
by Routledge
4 Park Square, Milton Park, Abingdon, Oxon OX14 4RN

and by Routledge
605 Third Avenue, New York, NY 10158

Routledge is an imprint of the Taylor & Francis Group, an informa business

© 2023 Sally-Ann Ashton

The right of Sally-Ann Ashton to be identified as author of this work has been asserted in accordance with sections 77 and 78 of the Copyright, Designs and Patents Act 1988.

Trademark notice: Product or corporate names may be trademarks or registered trademarks, and are used only for identification and explanation without intent to infringe.

British Library Cataloguing-in-Publication Data
A catalogue record for this book is available from the British Library

Library of Congress Cataloging-in-Publication Data
Names: Ashton, Sally-Ann, author.
Title: Pathways to adolescent male violent offending/Sally-Ann Ashton.
Description: First Edition. | New York, NY: Routledge, 2023. | Series: Routledge studies in criminal behaviour | Includes bibliographical references and index.
Identifiers: LCCN 2022061176 (print) | LCCN 2022061177 (ebook) |
ISBN 9781032186764 (hardback) | ISBN 9781032186771 (paperback) |
ISBN 9781003255697 (ebook)
Subjects: LCSH: Teenagers. | Adolescent psychology. | Criminal behavior.
Classification: LCC HQ797 .A78 2023 (print) | LCC HQ797 (ebook) |
DDC 305.235/1–dc23/eng/20230203
LC record available at https://lccn.loc.gov/2022061176
LC ebook record available at https://lccn.loc.gov/2022061177

ISBN: 978-1-032-18676-4 (hbk)
ISBN: 978-1-032-18677-1 (pbk)
ISBN: 978-1-003-25569-7 (ebk)

DOI: 10.4324/9781003255697

Typeset in Times New Roman
by Deanta Global Publishing Services, Chennai, India

For my parents Jacqui and Robin Ashton

Contents

Figures

Tables

Boxes

Acknowledgments

Firstly, I wish to acknowledge and thank the young people who shared their experiences. Their input was invaluable for understanding the risks that they face and their offending behaviors. The young people and the organization who took part in Study C cannot be named for reasons of anonymity. However, I am extremely grateful to all of those who took part and facilitated this study.

I am also grateful to the following organizations: Merseyside Police and partners, Greater Manchester Police, Salford Foundation, and Greater Manchester Combined Authorities.

At Salford Foundation I am grateful to Phil East, Sophie Sheehy, and Jack Ward for their patience and support. I also wish to acknowledge the work of Katharine Abbot, Greater Manchester Police.

I wish to thank Merseyside Police and the Merseyside Violence Reduction Partnership. I am grateful to Louise Kane and Paul Denn for their support. In particular, I recognize the contribution of Bonnie Chan and Michael Valentine; without their hard work it would not have been possible to undertake Study B.

Finally, special thanks to Wil Moran and my parents Jacqui and Robin Ashton for their encouragement and support.

Introduction

Box 0.1 represents a typical case study for adolescents who become involved in serious violent offending and organized crime as young adults (some details have been altered to ensure anonymity). The profile of the young person began with expressive violence in the company of others; this behavior continued

DOI: 10.4324/9781003255697-1

but also progressed to income-generating offenses during mid-adolescence, which progressed to involvement in county lines (the trafficking of drugs from cities to smaller towns). The history gives an idea of one route to involvement with organized crime, and it also serves as a reminder that offending trajectories and behaviors are dynamic in nature (Maguire & Bennett, 1982).

Background

The UK government's 2016 *Ending Gang Violence and Exploitation* strategy identified that gang involvement presents an increased risk of violence through drug selling, drug debts, and gang rivalries (HM Government, 2016). It also acknowledged the need for a multiagency approach to tackling and preventing violence at a local level and identified the use and dealing of drugs as a key driver of violence. The 2018 *Serious Violence Strategy* focused on county lines and the misuse of drugs as a driver of weapon use and homicide (HM Government, 2018). Recognizing the vulnerability of young people and advocating a multiagency public health approach (O'Moore, 2019) to tackle drugs and associated violence. The strategy recognized the need for early, targeted intervention and prevention, working with local communities, and a unified response across the criminal justice system (CJS). It also announced the launch of an Early Intervention Youth Fund (EIYF) for communities to tackle violent crime (HM Government, 2018). The exploitation of children in county lines operations and the association with weapon carrying are recognized (NCA, 2016, 2017). However, the process of adolescent criminal involvement is not as simple as is often described (NCA, 2020), and there is not a single route to being criminally exploited (Chapter 7).

The Box 0.1 case study demonstrates a common pathway from the early stages of expressive and reactive aggression to income-generating offenses, culminating in organized crime involvement. The early behaviors are not the root cause of escalation. This is the result of complex underlying factors that were present from early childhood, and which intensified over time. All young people who were among the most prolific arrestees in Study B witnessed domestic violence as a child, perpetrated by the father or male partner of the mother. In this subsample all young people had at least one parent and often an older male sibling with convictions for drug-related offenses (possession and sales). At least one family member had been a victim of violent crime. In a typical case from this subsample following an assessment by the youth offending service aged 17, the young person in Box 0.1 was recognized as vulnerable and easily manipulated by peers and vulnerable to criminal exploitation. He was also suspected of suffering from a behavioral, emotional, and social disorder (BESD) and of having attention deficit hyperactivity disorder (ADHD) but was not receiving any treatment. Involvement with organized crime and older offenders increased his risk of exposure to violence and psychological trauma. The normalization of criminal behaviors was present from an early age within his family and sustained by his later criminal associations.

Objectives and Summary

The objective of this book is to show a journey to involvement in serious violent crime. It will focus on standard information that is available to those who supervise and support young people in the justice system. It will demonstrate how that information can be used more effectively to understand behaviors and risk. Specifically, this book will differentiate between offending behaviors rather than approaching violence as a single entity. It will consider why some young people exhibit violent offending behaviors and will distinguish between those who use aggression expressively and those who use it for instrumental purposes. The book will explore key stages of adolescent offending with a view to early recognition of behaviors that leave young people vulnerable to criminal exploitation and the escalation of violence. In addition to recognizing traditional measurements of social and psychological risk, it stresses the importance of understanding crime motivations, how young people view themselves when they offend, and the emotions that they experience. Early adolescence is 11 to 13 years; middle adolescence is 14 to 16 years; and late adolescence is 17 to 19 years; early (or emerging) adulthood for purposes of this publication is defined as 18 to 25 years (Salmela-Aro, 2011). These categories are approximations, and it should be noted that individuals mature at different ages.

This book is the result of five years of UK-based research to understand how young people become involved in serious violence and organized crime. During this period, I had the opportunity to observe youth workers supporting young people as part of a behavioral program (Ashton & Ward, 2022), to advise on and evaluate the impact of one of the EIYF projects in Study A. As part of a parallel research project for Study B, I used historical youth offending supervision reports and police data to investigate child criminal exploitation and to understand the vulnerabilities associated with violent adolescent offenders (Ashton et al., 2021), subsequently examining the behaviors and risks associated with the most prolific arrestees from Study B. Finally, as part of an independent research project I interviewed young people for Study C, to understand their narratives of offending in groups (Ashton & Bussu, 2020; Ashton & Bussu, 2022; Ashton et al., forthcoming). Each source of data provided a novel perspective and revealed the stages and pathways to involvement in serious and organized crime.

Data Sources

Study A

Study A consisted of 119 males aged between 11 and 18 years, with an average age of 14.71. The young people were taking part in an intervention for those who were at risk of perpetrating or being a victim of a violent crime through association with peers, family, or associates who were involved in gangs or organized crime. Information was made available from the program referral risks and arrest data from the regional police database. A series of validated questionnaires were also utilized. The following measures were used: a version of a Self-Reported Offending questionnaire (Huizinga et al., 1991); Adolescent Drug Involvement Scale (Moberg & Hahn, 1991); the Mechanisms of Moral Disengagement Measure (Bandura et al., 1991); and an amended version of the Youth Psychopathic Traits Inventory (YPI; Andershed et al., 2002) considers three traits: grandiose manipulative dimension, callous-unemotional dimension, and impulsive irresponsible dimension. The rationale for including the moral disengagement and psychopathic traits measures was to compare questionnaires before and after the community intervention program. It was not to label the young people as "psychopathic"; rather, this scale represented observed traits that presented a risk for problematic behaviors and grooming by criminal gangs (Ashton & Ward, 2022).

Study B

Study B consisted of 172 males who were between 12 and 18 years of age at the first point of contact with a Youth Offending Team (YOT) and were an average age of 16 years (standard deviation 1.37 years); 80.1% (N = 141) of the male sample identified as White British; 7% (N = 12) as Mixed "other background"; 5.9% (N = 10) as White "other"; 1.8% (N = 3) as Asian/White mixed; 2.9% (N = 5) as Black "other"; and 0.6% (N = 1) as: Black British Caribbean, Mixed Black Caribbean/White; Mixed Black African/White; Mixed "any other background".

Data for this sample came from three sources. First, historical AssetPlus forms, used as part of the YOT assessment and management of children and young people who are under their supervision (YJB, 2014). The AssetPlus records focus on information gathering in the following areas: personal, family, and social factors (professional risk and protective factor assessments); offending and antisocial behavior; foundations for change; self-assessment (YJB, 2022). A recent evaluation of the AssetPlus assessments concluded that the current system does not fully reflect the Child First Strategy (YJB, 2019). Assessments are undertaken for different purposes and for some young people at multiple points. These include supervision for restorative justice, referral order reports, pre-sentencing reports, custody reports, referral reports, bail, and remand, leaving custody, transfer to a different YOT, and transfer from youth to adult services. Following an initial assessment young people can be required to undertake specialist modules (for example substance use). Second, a regional police database containing information relating to local police callouts and their outcomes. These records indicate the location of offense and list any co-offenders. They also report victimization, including early callouts for domestic violence (DV). From the total sample 22 young people had a significantly higher number of arrests. Their histories were explored in more detail, including their co-offending networks and family involvement in crime. The relationship between family criminal history and youth offending can be complex and indirect (Farrington, 2010). Nevertheless, significant direct and indirect associations between family criminal involvement and the most prolific arrestees were found.

The two samples are referred to as Study B total sample and Study B subsample. Ashton and colleagues (2021) published the research findings on categories of violent offender for the total sample.

Study C

Study C consisted of 20 participants who were purposively recruited from a group of 12- to 17-year-old males (with an average age of 15.55 and a standard deviation of 1.20 years) who had been referred to a community-based behavioral program in Northern England. To be included in the program the young people had to be at risk of/involved in gangs or to have committed a violent offense. Part of this research focused on how participants experienced offending with other people (Ashton et al., forthcoming). They were asked to describe a crime that they committed with other people and then completed a 36-item roles questionnaire and the 26-item emotions questionnaire (Ioannou et al., 2017) with the offense in mind (see Chapter 1). The results of this analysis are published in a forthcoming paper (Ashton et al., forthcoming). Ashton and Bussu (2020) published a qualitative analysis of the different types of offending groups that were identified by the young people in the sample. They published a second paper (Ashton & Bussu, 2022) on the roles and motivations of young people who co-offend.

Approach

Adopting an (investigative) psychological framework (Canter & Youngs, 2009) this book differentiates between categories of adolescent offending and explores the behavioral and social profiles of those who commit violent acts. Although this applied field of psychology is traditionally associated with criminal investigations, researchers have contributed extensively to our understanding of offender characteristics and behaviors (Canter, 1994, 1995; Canter & Alison, 1997; Canter & Youngs, 2009). Key to this approach is using statistical behavioral patterns to understanding criminal actions and what these tell us about the offender (Canter & Youngs, 2009). These methods have been used successfully to differentiate between categories of offender for individual categories of violent offenses such as arson (Canter & Fritzon, 1998), homicide (Trojan & Salfati, 2016), burglary (Fox et al., 2020), and robbery (Burrell, 2022), based on the premise that people commit the same categories of offense for different reasons, motivations, and circumstances. The findings offer a crucial insight into where to focus interventions and programs for young people who exhibit aggressive and violent behavior. This approach works equally well for understanding common patterns of risk associated with offending, still taking account of individual factors that influence involvement in crime.

Investigative psychology uses multidimensional scaling techniques to explore behavioral patterns. This book uses smallest space analysis, a form of multidimensional scaling, to explore the relationship between behavioral and risk variables. Smallest space analysis (SSA) calculates the interrelationship between variables and produces the smallest dimensionality among these (Fox et al., 2020). This produces a correlation matrix which is transformed into a rank-ordered three-dimensional plot. The variables that commonly occur together are positioned in the same region of the output in the form of a plot (Canter & Youngs, 2009; Fox et al., 2020). The division of the plot is determined by the researcher and is based on empirical evidence.

Filling in the Gaps

The three studies utilize a range of data sources including professional risk assessments, arrest records, supervision records, and self-reported attitudinal and behavioral scales. All three cohorts were made up of young people who had committed at least one violent act or who were at risk or gang involvement. Each study utilized different methods of data collection; however, every approach presents a potential bias. Arrest records are unlikely to represent every offense that an individual commits. Equally someone may be arrested and not have been involved. Some young people may embellish their self-reported offending for social gain, especially when speaking to a researcher, or they may not feel comfortable admitting to involvement with certain types of offenses (compare Thornberry et al., 2003). For this reason, the self-reported and official offending records for Study A were triangulated to see if they corresponded. In most cases greater numbers and

Table 0.1 Study A: Official and self-reported offending

ID	Official	Self-reported
694	Burglary, antisocial behavior, arson with intent to endanger life and burglary; criminal damage, assault, theft	Criminal damage, arson, burglary, shoplifting, handling stolen goods, theft of a motor vehicle, sold cannabis, fighting
713	Criminal damage, assault	Criminal damage, arson, handled stolen goods, robbery without a weapon, fighting, gang fight, carried a weapon
913	Criminal damage, theft of a motor vehicle, theft, theft from a motor vehicle, motoring offenses, aggravated vehicle taking, possession of cannabis, shoplifting, robbery, burglary	Joyriding, theft of a motor vehicle, assault, fighting, gang fight

more variation of offenses were reported by the young people compared to the official records. However, there were some exceptions to this. Table 0.1 shows that 913 had been charged more times than his own account. The only crime for which there was no further action was aggravated vehicle taking; the victim identified the young person as the perpetrator but did not support charges. It is of course possible that he did not commit the offense.

Both self-reported and arrest/charge data offer a useful overview of the types of behaviors that a young person engages in. Police records can also offer a summary of the offense itself and the role that the young person fulfilled. Motivation, emotions, and roles can be inferred from some of these records, but any subsequent interview with a young person who has committed a crime is likely to be impacted by its official nature, especially for young people who are involved in organized crime or who are fearful of repercussions if they speak in any detail about the offense or co-offenders. Importantly, Study C used a criminal narratives approach to explore how young people who offend with other people experience the planning and commissioning of a crime. This research also identified that young people distinguish between peer groups, street gangs, and involvement in organized criminal groups (Ashton & Bussu, 2020).

Aggression and Violence

The terms "aggression" and "violence" are not used uniformly by researchers. Although some social psychologists define aggression as an intentional behavior with the purpose of harming someone either physically or psychologically (Allen & Anderson, 2017), not all agree that intention is a necessary component (Loeber & Hay, 1997). Social psychologists generally identify violence as an extreme type of aggression that is aimed at a person (Allen & Anderson, 2017). Many researchers discount the damage of inanimate objects as a form of aggression (Krahé, 2020), whereas others include acts such as criminal damage if the overall intention is to harm another person (Parrott & Giancola, 2007). For the purposes of the current publication, with its focus on offending behaviors, damaging property intentionally is considered as an act of aggression, because it can be used reactively, as an act of defiance or revenge, or with the intention of threatening or intimidating the victim. Psychologists distinguish between hostile aggression which is the result of anger and has the aim of causing harm or injury and instrumental aggression, which serves a purpose other than causing pain (Berkowitz, 1993). Assault, for example, may fall into either category depending on the trigger or motivation of an individual. An argument might provoke feelings of anger and cause someone to physically attack the other person (hostile) or could be a means of gaining social credibility within a group.

Self-control (Gottfredson & Hirschi, 1990) can be a particular challenge for some young people and is associated with risk-taking, thrill seeking, and reactive aggression (Steinberg, 2010; Vaughan et al., 2019; Wojciechowski, 2020). One young person who was interviewed for Study C reflected on his inability to control his reactive anger and how this had caused him to act violently during his early adolescence. Such responses can change as a person moves from early adolescence (11 to 14) to mid-adolescence (15 to 17) into late adolescence (18 to 21). However, research has indicated that some males do not fully develop impulse control until they reach their mid-20s (Shulman et al., 2015).

Youth violence refers to violence that occurs among individuals aged 10–29 years who are unrelated and who may or may not know each other. It generally takes place outside of the home. It includes a range of acts from bullying and physical fighting to more severe sexual and physical assault, to homicide (Krug et al., 2002). The term "juvenile delinquency" can also incorporate acts of aggression or violence, but it is used more generally as a legal definition for a minor who offends (Allen & Anderson, 2017). However, some researchers use this term for minor offenses or early offending behaviors. Antisocial behavior is another activity that is associated with young people and is a common early arrest for early adolescents from the studies cited above. Behavior is deemed antisocial if it violates social norms and can include aggression and violent acts (DeWall & Anderson, 2011).

Coercion is defined as an action to force compliance through threats, punishment, or physical force (Tedeschi & Felson, 1994) and in this form can be considered a form of instrumental aggression. The coercion and exploitation of young people by drug gangs and county lines operators employs violence but also psychological abuse of a similar type that is associated with child sexual exploitation (Ashton & Bussu, 2020). Several young people in Study C described a process that is associated with the sexual exploitation of children to coerce them into selling and trafficking drugs (Cockbain, 2013 for discussion of CSE grooming in the UK). Early contact involved giving the young people gifts (clothes, drugs, alcohol, access to cars). The adults then seek to distance the young person from their family by taking them to different areas or regions in an expensive car, letting the young person see how much "respect" the adult is shown by others. This social process is something that appeals to young people, and social status is cited as an incentive to offend with peers (Warr, 2022). Adult gang members then test the young person who they are seeking to recruit by asking them to hold or move illegal items or to become involved in violence. One participant described being asked to load a shotgun, which was then used to harm a rival adult gang member. He was naturally traumatized by this experience and was reminded that he was now complicit in a serious criminal act. All of those who had been involved with criminal gangs described being beaten and abused during the early stages of their involvement. This method works to trauma-bond the young person to the group (Sanchez et al., 2019). When trauma bonding occurs, the victim is isolated from other people's perspectives; they associate leaving with danger and believe that there is no escape from their situation. If a young person has been excluded from school and their parents are not able to offer support at home, they can become even more vulnerable to criminal exploitation (Pitts, 2007).

Exposure to violence includes being either a witness or a victim of a violent act; the exposure can be recent or over a lifetime (Dodge et al., 1990). Two specific categories of serious violence were identified as an increased risk for those between the ages of 10 and 17 years in England (Kincaid et al., 2019). First, becoming a victim of a robbery or sexual assault, with or without injury; and second, the heightened risk associated with knife or weapon carrying. The authors estimated that the number of young people who had experienced serious violence could be six times greater than reported victimization (Kincaid et al., 2019; NCA, 2018). There are strong associations between exposure to violence and mental disorders, which can then increase an individual's risk of violent offending (Flannery et al., 2006; 2001). Violent victimization is also associated with reduced impulse control during adolescence (Monahan et al., 2013). For some young people exposure to violence begins in the home. Domestic violence (DV) can impact a developing child in two ways. Witnessing aggressive responses and violent behavior and feeling threatened is traumatic for anyone, particularly a child who has no means of leaving the situation. Aggressive behavior can also become a learned response if family members respond to situations with aggression as part of a "cognitive script" that becomes reinforced by achieving a desired outcome (Bandura, 1973, 1979). For young people who become involved in gangs and/or serious organized crime the risk of witnessing violence and/or victimization is increased (Ashton & Ioannou, 2022).

Data Sources

Youth offending assessments report professional and self-assessed risk, giving young people the opportunity to reflect and share. Ashton and colleagues (2021) looked specifically at the relationship between risk and three violent offenses of assault, robbery, and knife carrying for Study B total sample. Knife crime was not associated with any specific risks. Assault was associated with domestic violence callouts, history or violence, substance use, low school attendance, and inappropriate use of time. Robbery, on the other hand, was linked with family criminal involvement, social risks, groomed by peers, gang involvement, and having an influence over peers. The associated psychological risks were numerous: ADHD, special educational needs, PTSD, victim of abuse. These manifested in self-harm, anxiety, depression, and were also linked to the risk of drug debt. When young people under supervision were asked about associated risk the extent of the underlying issues was even clearer. Knife carrying and assault were associated with problems with school, feeling angry and stressed, not thinking about consequences. As with the professional assessment, robbery was associated with additional psychological problems. These included self-harm, suicidal thoughts, drinking too much, drugs, problems at home, and missing from home. The protective factors were more closely associated with expressive violence, whereas for those who had been arrested for robbery there were significant and complex areas where the young people would require additional support.

Referral records for a community program for Study A contained a short dichotomous list of behavioral (antisocial/criminal behavior, violent or coercive, intel on weapon carrying, missing from home), familial (parent in prison, CJS, family violence, child protection plan, looked after child status), and educational (exclusion or disengagement). Figure 0.1 shows the relationship between these risks (as present) and self-reported offenses. One striking difference is the placement of intelligence and self-reported weapon carrying. This can partly be explained by a 16% difference in that 60% of the sample reported weapon carrying compared to 44% cited in the risk assessment. As with the referral risks from Study A, self-reported weapon carrying was associated with expressive violence. Also in this region were criminal behavior, social risks, school exclusions, and child protection plan in place. The other offenses were fighting, destroying property, and assault.

Family risk was on the right side of the plot, and as with Study B, these were associated with income-generating crimes of robbery, burglary, drug sales, handling stolen goods, shoplifting, and illegal use of a credit card. Also in this region were theft of a motor vehicle and joyriding, which support the findings in Study C and the link between these offenses and involvement in organized crime.

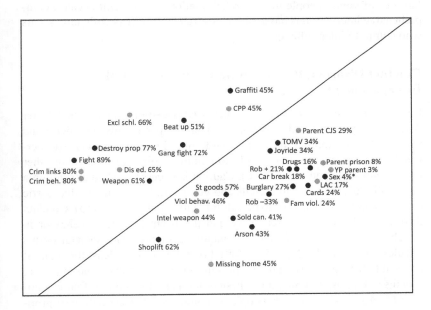

Figure 0.1 Study A: The relationship between risk and self-reported offending Coefficient of alienation = 0.10.

Key: Gray = professional risk and Black = offending. CPP = child protection plan in place; dis ed. = disengaged from education; excl schl. = school exclusion; rob = robbery plus (+) and minus (−) a weapon; cards = used a credit card illegally; fam viol. = history of family violence; st goods = handling stolen goods; TOMV = theft of a motor vehicle; YP parent = young person is a parent; crim beh. = history of criminal and antisocial behavior. *Sexual offenses were recorded from official data only.

In essence the different data sources (police arrest data, supervision records, professional assessments, self-reported risk) tell the same story. The family plays a pivotal role in increased risk or protection, and for this reason they should be included in any intervention (Henggeler et al., 1992; Marcus, 2017). As demonstrated, the family can present a criminogenic and behavioral risk for young people. However, families can also be in a state of crisis on account of an adolescent's behavior and feel at a loss in terms of how to support them. It is worth noting that the studies in this book consist of young people who were already at the stage of violent offending. For such cohorts the home environment and family presented a distinct risk. This would suggest that programs need to include support for families and to ensure that any interventions are followed through at home. Including the families of young people in their rehabilitation is important because comprehensive interventions have the highest rates of success with adolescents who commit violent offences.

Conduct Disorder, Psychopathic Traits, and Moral Disengagement

Research has indicated that adolescents who exhibit traits from Cluster A (for example paranoid, schizoid, schizotypal personality disorders) and Cluster B (for example antisocial, borderline, histrionic, narcissistic personality disorders) are more likely to commit violent offenses than other adolescents (Johnson et al., 2000). Caution is necessary when attributing a personality disorder to adolescents and young adults, and many diagnostic criteria require the behavior to be exhibited in adulthood (*DSM 5*). Conduct disorder is defined as "a repetitive and persistent pattern of behavior in which the basic rights of others or major age-appropriate societal norms or rules are violated" (*DSM 5*, p. 469). For a diagnosis, at least three out of a possible fifteen criteria must be present, including at least one in the six months before the examination. These criteria are divided into four categories: (1) Aggression towards people and animals; (2) Destruction of property; (3) Deceitfulness or theft; (4) Serious violations of rules. ADHD and oppositional defiant disorder can co-occur with conduct disorder (*DSM 5*), and there are other disorders with similar behaviors that can be confused with a diagnosis. Psychological illness and disorders are treatable in adolescents and a diagnosis can also help a young person make sense of behaviors over which they have little or no control. It is essential that a diagnosis is made by a qualified practitioner rather than noting that a young person may have A or B on account of their behavior. Additionally, it is important to understand whether a young person acts alone or is influenced by external factors such as family, peers, or older criminals.

Psychopathy (Murphy & Vess, 2003) represents a combination of recognized personality disorders and can be categorized by subtypes of antisocial, narcissistic, borderline, and sadistic in adult samples (*DSM 5*) and is only diagnosed in adults. For antisocial personality disorder to be diagnosed, conduct disorder needs to have been present. However, not every young person with a diagnosis of conduct disorder goes on to develop antisocial personality disorder (Offord & Bennett, 1994). Most young people age out of their behavior. Several studies on juvenile gang membership and violent offending have included measures for psychopathic traits, which are dynamic during adolescence (Ashton, 2018; Ashton & Ward, 2022; Cauffman et al., 2016). A study of instrumental and reactive violent adult offenders found differences in their psychopathic scores (Cornell et al., 1996). The authors found instrumental offenders to be more superficial, manipulative, callous, and impulsive than their reactive violent counterparts.

There are several measures for psychopathic traits in young people. The PCL-YV, a youth version of Hare's interview-based PCL-R for adults (Forth et al., 2003), requires trained assessors to code and assess results. There are other scale-based questionnaires such as the Youth Psychopathic Traits Inventory (Andershed et al., 2002). This measures three personality traits: grandiose manipulative dimension, callous unemotional dimension, and impulsive irresponsible dimension. Research has indicated that psychopathy is dynamic in adolescence, it is common for both lay persons and practitioners to misunderstand psychopathy (Berg et al., 2013). Research has found a correlation between higher psychopathic traits and offending frequencies for adolescent offenders (Dyck et al., 2013). Callousness and unemotionality are associated with high levels of antisocial behaviors among incarcerated youth (Silverthorne et al., 2001) and general populations of adolescents (Essau et al., 2006). They have been linked to increased group offending and gang membership (Thornton et al., 2015). Researchers have also found that high levels of callous-unemotional traits were associated with an increase in violence and substance use, while controlling for environmental factors (Baskin-Sommers et al., 2015). Empathy has also been found to be a protective risk factor against involvement in criminal activities (Morgado & Vale-Dias, 2013). In a study on the relationship between peer delinquency and psychopathy, the authors (Kerr et al., 2012) question how the three dimensions of psychopathy (Cooke & Michie, 2001) might influence interactions with others in offending groups. The study found that individuals who scored highly on the callous-unemotional and grandiose manipulative dimensions had a greater influence over others and higher resistance to peer influence.

Moral Disengagement

Social cognitive theory suggests that most individuals do not transgress the law because they have internalized societal standards of conduct, and thus criminal or harmful behavior not only risks legal sanctions but also impacts negatively upon their concept of moral self (Bandura, 1999). Bandura suggested that to avoid feelings of shame or guilt individuals rationalize their behavior in a process that he identified as moral disengagement. The moral attitudes of young people have been shown to be more influenced by their peers from early adolescence (Caravita et al., 2013). However, research has also indicated that individuals with traits such as grandiosity, manipulation, and callousness also exhibit higher levels of such disengagement (Dhingra et al., 2015). These research findings therefore suggest that changing attitudes to transgressing societal pro-social norms and law breaking require an understanding of peer or group norms and individual characteristics. Adolescent males have been found to use moral disengagement to justify behavior (Elvira De Caroli & Sagone, 2014). A decrease in moral disengagement is a longer-term protective factor for young people and is particularly relevant for those who offend in groups. Even among adult career offenders there are certain crimes that they would not wish to be associated with, for example, sexual offenses.

Research has consistently shown that the peak age for most offenses is late adolescence (see for example Hirschi & Gottfredson, 1983, 1988; Farrington, 1986; Moffitt, 1993). There are both social (Farrington, 1986) and developmental (Loeber et al., 2012) explanations for this phenomenon. There are both individual and group influences on adolescent offending and desistance. The present publication seeks to understand the complexities of background factors that are associated with the escalation from offenses that are commonly committed by early adolescents to serious violent offending and involvement with organized criminal groups.

Relationship between Risk and Offending

Police records probably contain the most comprehensive account of family behavior and risk. As noted earlier in this chapter, the young people who had become prolific arrestees during mid-adolescence (Study B subsample) all had at least one convicted family member (Table 0.2). Typically, these included violence and income-generating crimes. Many of their parents were also listed as vulnerable adults, with substance use, addiction, mental illness, and criminal victimization listed for mothers and fathers. Stepfathers posed an added risk for their new families with domestic violence, involvement in organized crime, and drug use

Table 0.2 Study B subsample: Risk factors

Risk factor	Yes N	Yes %	No N	No %
Family criminal record				
Mother	16	76.2	5	23.8
Father	13	76.5	4	23.5
Sibling	15	71.4	6	71.4
Other family	11	50	11	50
In care ever	12	54.5	10	45.5
Early DV callouts	20	95.2	1	4.8
Psychological disorders				
ADHD	12	54.5	10	45.5
BESD	5	22.7	5	77.3
ODD	2	9.1	2	90.9
Autism spectrum disorder	2	9.1	2	90.9
Mood disorder	4	18.2	4	81.8
Any disorder present	17	77.3	5	22.7

commonly listed on their arrest records. Two further male influences were in this region (Figure 0.2): other family member with a criminal record and an older co-arrestee. A diagnosis of ADHD also presented an additional behavioral risk for half of the sample, particularly because notes often indicated that the young person was not on medication to support their condition. A review of the literature revealed there is insufficient evidence to support a causal relationship between ADHD and prenatal risk (Scriberras et al., 2017). ADHD can be partly explained by genetics, in that there tend to be others in the immediate family who suffer from this disorder (Kian et al., 2022). These researches have recognized that young people who suffer from ADHD are disadvantaged in both educational and youth justice contexts, even though they are overrepresented in the justice system (Day, 2021).

In the right region of the plot, mothers with a criminal record related to a sibling who offended, being placed in care, anxiety/depression, and class A drug use. Records showed that mothers often had convictions for drug use and were noted as suffering from mental illness, making the parenting of a young person who was exhibiting signs of behavioral problems impossible in some cases. The result was that the young person was placed in care. Thus, Table 0.2 effectively demonstrates how generational trauma can impact a young person's behavior and potential (Halsey, 2018).

Summary and Implications for Practice

Box 0.1 illustrated the complex nature of typical cases of enhanced adolescent violence and involvement with adult criminal gangs. It is necessary to

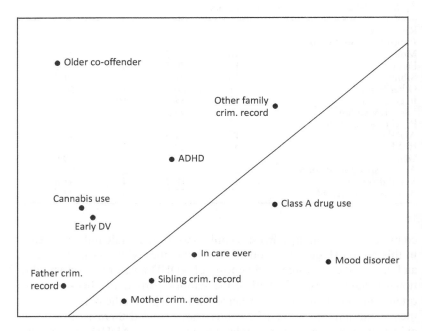

Figure 0.2 Study B subsample: The relationship between risk factors
Coefficient of alienation = 0.05.

look at a comprehensive picture of behavior rather than a single offense. Police datasets are in a unique position to provide a snapshot of behavioral and social risks over multiple generations. Family can act as either a protective or a risk factor in a young person's life. It is essential for family to be involved in any intervention to support a young person, irrespective of their relationship to his behavior. In the cases of the young people who had been arrested the most, there was evidence of generational trauma, victimization, and violent behavior among parents. For this reason, families with callouts for domestic violence need to be supported and the impact of exposure to violence for children and young people in the family unit needs to be considered when assessing problematic behavior. Excluding young people from school for behavioral reasons adds to their vulnerability to criminal exploitation and removes a source of pro-social support. Psychological assessments are necessary if educational and criminal justice practitioners are to be able to support young people effectively, and they can also help a young person to understand their responses and behaviors.

References

Allen, J. J., & Anderson, C. A. (2017). Aggression and violence: Definitions and distinctions. In P. Sturmey (Ed.), *The Wiley handbook of violence and aggression* (pp. 1–14). John Wiley & Sons, Ltd.

American Psychiatric Association. (2013). *Diagnostic and statistical manual of mental disorders* (5th ed.). https://doi.org/10.1176/appi.books.9780890425596

Andershed, H. A., Kerr, M., Stattin, H., & Levander, S. (2002). Psychopathic traits in non-referred youths: A new assessment tool. In E. Blaauw & L. Sheridan (Eds.), *Psychopaths: Current international perspectives* (pp. 131–158). Elsevier.

Ashton, S. A., & Bussu, A. (2020). Peer groups, street gangs and organised crime in the narratives of adolescent male offenders. *Journal of Criminal Psychology*, *10*(4), 277–292.

Ashton, S.-A., & Bussu, A. (2022). The social dynamics of adolescent co-offending. *Youth Justice*, *17*(3).

Ashton, S.-A., Ioannou, M., & Hammond, L. (forthcoming). Applying the criminal narrative roles and emotions to young people who offend in groups.

Ashton, S. A., Valentine, M., & Chan, B. (2021). Differentiating categories of violent adolescent offending and the associated risks in police and youth offending service records. *International Journal of Offender Therapy and Comparative Criminology*.

Ashton, S.-A., & Ward, J. (2022). Bridging the gap between criminal psychology and frontline youthwork: A case study in programme development and evaluation. *Assessment and Development Matters*, *14*(4), 15–20.

Bandura, A. (1973). *Aggression: A social learning analysis*. Prentice-Hall.

Bandura, A. (1979). Self-referent mechanisms in social learning theory. *American Psychologist*, *34*(5), 439–441.

Bandura, A. (1999). Social cognitive theory of personality. In D. Cervone & Y. Shoda (Eds.), *The coherence of personality: Social-cognitive bases of consistency, variability, and organization* (pp. 185–241).

Baskin-Sommers, A. R., Curtin, J. J., & Newman, J. P. (2015). Altering the cognitive-affective dysfunctions of psychopathic and externalizing offender subtypes with cognitive remediation. *Clinical Psychological Science*, *3*(1), 45–57.

Berg, J. M., Smith, S. F., Watts, A. L., Ammirati, R., Green, S. E., & Lilienfeld, S. O. (2013). Misconceptions regarding psychopathic personality: Implications for clinical practice and research. *Neuropsychiatry*, *3*(1), 63–74.

Berkowitz, L. (1993). *Aggression: Its causes, consequences, and control*. Mcgraw-Hill Book Company.

Burrell, A. (2022). *Robbery*. Palgrave Macmillan.

Canter, D. (1995). Psychology of offender profiling. In R. Bull & D. Carson (Eds.), *Handbook of psychology in legal contexts* (pp. 343–355). John Wiley & Sons Ltd.

Canter, D., & Fritzon, K. (1998). Differentiating arsonists: A model of firesetting actions and characteristics. *Legal and Criminological Psychology*, *3*(1), 73–96.

Canter, D. V. (1994). *Criminal shadows: Inside the mind of the serial killer* (pp. 63–69). HarperCollins.

Canter, D. V., & Alison, L. J. (Eds.). (1997). *Criminal detection and the psychology of crime*. Dartmouth Publishing Company.

Canter, D. V., & Youngs, D. (2009). *Investigative psychology: Offender profiling and the analysis of criminal action*. John Wiley & Sons.

Cauffman, E., Skeem, J., Dmitrieva, J., & Cavanagh, C. (2016). Comparing the stability of psychopathy scores in adolescents versus adults: How often is "fledgling psychopathy" misdiagnosed? *Psychology, Public Policy, and Law*, *22*(1), 77–91.

Cockbain, E. (2013). Grooming and the 'Asian sex gang predator': The construction of a racial crime threat. *Race and Class*, *54*(4), 22–32.

Cooke, D. J., & Michie, C. (2001). Refining the construct of psychopathy: Towards a hierarchical model. *Psychological Assessment*, *13*(2), 171–188.

Cornell, D. G., Warren, J., Hawk, G., Stafford, E., Oram, G., & Pine, D. (1996). Psychopathy in instrumental and reactive violent offenders. *Journal of Consulting and Clinical Psychology*, *64*(4), 783–790.

De Caroli, M. E., & Sagone, E. (2014). Belief in a just world, prosocial behavior, and moral disengagement in adolescence. *Procedia-Social and Behavioral Sciences*, *116*, 596–600.

DeWall, C. N., & Anderson, C. A. (2011). The general aggression model. In P. R. Shaver & M. Mikulincer (Eds.), *Human aggression and violence: Causes, manifestations, and consequences* (pp. 15–33). American Psychological Association.

Dhingra, K., Debowska, A., Sharratt, K., Hyland, P., & Kola-Palmer, S. (2015). Psychopathy, gang membership, and moral disengagement among juvenile offenders. *Journal of Criminal Psychology*, *5*(1), 13–24.

Dodge, K. A., Bates, J. E., & Pettit, G. S. (1990). Mechanisms in the cycle of violence. *Science*, *250*(4988), 1678–1683.

Dyck, H. L., Campbell, M. A., Schmidt, F., & Wershler, J. L. (2013). Youth psychopathic traits and their impact on long-term criminal offending trajectories. *Youth Violence and Juvenile Justice*, *11*(3), 230–248.

Essau, C. A., Sasagawa, S., & Frick, P. J. (2006). Callous-unemotional traits in a community sample of adolescents. *Assessment*, *13*(4), 454–469.

Farrington, D. P. (1986). Age and crime. *Crime and Justice*, *7*, 189–250.

Farrington, D. P. (2010). The developmental evidence base: Psychosocial research. In G. J. Towl & D. A. Crighton (Eds.), *Forensic psychology* (pp. 113–132). Wiley Blackwell.

Flannery, D. J., Singer, M. I., & Wester, K. (2001). Violence exposure, psychological trauma, and suicide risk in a community sample of dangerously violent adolescents. *Journal of the American Academy of Child and Adolescent Psychiatry*, *40*(4), 435–442.

Forth, A. E., Kosson, D. S., & Hare, R. D. (2003). *Hare psychopathy checklist: Youth version*. Multi-Health Systems.

Fox, B., Farrington, D. P., Kapardis, A., & Hambly, O. C. (2020). *Evidence-based offender profiling*. Routledge.

Halsey, M. (2018). Child victims as adult offenders: Foregrounding the criminogenic effects of (unresolved) trauma and loss. *British Journal of Criminology*, *58*(1), 17–36.

Henggeler, S. W., Melton, G. B., & Smith, L. A. (1992). Family preservation using multisystemic therapy: An effective alternative to incarcerating serious juvenile offenders. *Journal of Consulting and Clinical Psychology*, *60*(6), 953–961.

Hirschi, T., & Gottfredson, M. (1983). Age and the explanation of crime. *American Journal of Sociology*, *89*(3), 552–584.

Hirschi, T., & Gottfredson, M. (1988). Towards a general theory of crime. In W. Buikhuisen & S. A. Mednick (Eds.), *Explaining criminal behaviour: Interdisciplinary approaches* (pp. 8–26). Brill Sense.

HM Government. (2016). *Ending gang violence and exploitation*. HM Government.

HM Government. (2018). *Serious violence strategy*. HM Government.

Huizinga, D., Esbensen, F. A., & Weiher, A. W. (1991). Are there multiple paths to delinquency. *Journal of Criminal Law and Criminology*, *82*(1), 83–118.

Johnson, J. G., Cohen, P., Kasen, S., Skodol, A. E., Hamagami, F., & Brook, J. S. (2000). Age-related change in personality disorder trait levels between early adolescence and adulthood: A community-based longitudinal investigation. *Acta Psychiatrica Scandinavica*, *102*(4), 265–275.

Kerr, M., Van Zalk, M., & Stattin, H. (2012). Psychopathic traits moderate peer influence on adolescent delinquency. *Journal of Child Psychology and Psychiatry*, *53*(8), 826–835.

Kincaid, S., du Mont, S., Tipple, C., & Desroches, C. (2019). Serious violence in context: Understanding the scale and nature of serious violence. A Report by Crest Advisory.

Krahé, B. (2020). *The social psychology of aggression*. Routledge.

Krug, E. G., Mercy, J. A., Dahlberg, L. L., & Zwi, A. B. (2002). The world report on violence and health. *Lancet*, *360*(9339), 1083–1088.

Loeber, R., & Hay, D. (1997). Key issues in the development of aggression and violence from childhood to early adulthood. *Annual Review of Psychology*, *48*(1), 371–410.

Loeber, R., Menting, B., Lynam, D. R., Moffitt, T. E., Stouthamer-Loeber, M., Stallings, R., Farrington, D. P., & Pardini, D. (2012). Findings from the Pittsburgh youth study: Cognitive impulsivity and intelligence as predictors of the age–crime curve. *Journal of the American Academy of Child and Adolescent Psychiatry*, *51*(11), 1136–1149.

Maguire, M., & Bennett, T. (1982). *Burglary in a dwelling: The offence, the offender and the victim*. Heinemann.

Marcus, R. F. (2017). *The development of aggression and violence in adolescence*. Palgrave Macmillan.

Moberg, D. P., & Hahn, L. (1991). The adolescent drug involvement scale. *Journal of Child and Adolescent Substance Abuse*, *2*(1), 75–88.

Moffitt, T. E. (1993). The neuropsychology of conduct disorder. *Development and Psychopathology*, *5*(1–2), 135–151.

Monahan, K. C., Steinberg, L., Cauffman, E., & Mulvey, E. P. (2013). Psychosocial (im) maturity from adolescence to early adulthood: Distinguishing between adolescence-limited and persisting antisocial behavior. *Development and Psychopathology*, *25*(4pt1), 1093–1105.

Morgado, A. M., & da Luz Vale-Dias, M. (2013). The antisocial phenomenon in adolescence: What is literature telling us? *Aggression and Violent Behavior*, *18*(4), 436–443.

Murphy, C., & Vess, J. (2003). Subtypes of psychopathy: Proposed differences between narcissistic, borderline, sadistic, and antisocial psychopaths. *Psychiatric Quarterly*, *74*(1), 11–29.

NCA. (2016). *National strategic assessment of serious and organised crime 2016*. National Crime Agency.

NCA. (2017). *County lines violence, exploitation & drug supply 2017*. National Crime Agency.

NCA. (2020). *National strategic assessment of serious and organised crime 2020*. National Crime Agency.

O'Moore, É. (2019). *A whole-system multi-agency approach to serious violence prevention: A resource for local system leaders in England*. Public Health England.

Offord, D. R., & Bennett, K. J. (1994). Conduct disorder: Long-term outcomes and intervention effectiveness. *Journal of the American Academy of Child and Adolescent Psychiatry*, *33*(8), 1069–1078.

Parrott, D. J., & Giancola, P. R. (2007). Addressing "the criterion problem" in the assessment of aggressive behavior: Development of a new taxonomic system. *Aggression and Violent Behavior*, *12*(3), 280–299.

Salmela-Aro, K. (2011). Stages of adolescence. In B. Bradford Brown & M.J. Prinstein (Eds.), *Encyclopedia of adolescence* (pp. 360–368). Academic Press.

Sanchez, R. V., Speck, P. M., & Patrician, P. A. (2019). A concept analysis of trauma coercive bonding in the commercial sexual exploitation of children. *Journal of Pediatric Nursing*, *46*, 48–54.

Sciberras, E., Mulraney, M., Silva, D., & Coghill, D. (2017). Prenatal risk factors and the etiology of ADHD—Review of existing evidence. *Current Psychiatry Reports*, *19*(1), 1–8.

Silverthorn, P., Frick, P. J., & Reynolds, R. (2001). Timing of onset and correlates of severe conduct problems in adjudicated girls and boys. *Journal of Psychopathology and Behavioral Assessment*, *23*(3), 171–181.

Steinberg, L. (2010). A dual systems model of adolescent risk-taking. *Developmental Psychobiology: The Journal of the International Society for Developmental Psychobiology*, *52*(3), 216–224.

Tedeschi, J. T., & Felson, R. B. (1994). *Violence, aggression, and coercive actions*. American Psychological Association.

Thornberry, T. P., Krohn, M. D., Lizotte, A. J., Smith, C. A., & Tobin, K. (2003). *Gangs and delinquency in developmental perspective* (Kindle Version ed.). Cambridge University Press.

Thornton, L. C., Frick, P. J., Shulman, E. P., Ray, J. V., Steinberg, L., & Cauffman, E. (2015). Callous-unemotional traits and adolescents' role in group crime. *Law and Human Behavior*, *39*(4), 368–377.

Trojan, C., & Salfati, G. (2016). Criminal history of homicide offenders: A multidimensional analysis of criminal specialization. *Journal of Criminal Psychology*, *5*(3), 125–145.

Vaughan, T. J., Ward, J. T., Bouffard, J., & Piquero, A. R. (2019). The general factor of self-control and cost consideration: A critical test of the general theory of crime. *Crime and Delinquency*, *65*(6), 731–771.

Wojciechowski, T. (2020). The relevance of the dual systems model of self-control for age-related deceleration in offending variety among juvenile offenders. *Journal of Criminal Justice*, *70*, 101716.

YJB. (2014). *AssetPlus: Assessment and planning in the youth justice system*. Youth Justice Board for England and Wales.

YJB. (2022). *AssetPlus outcome evaluation: Final report*. Youth Justice Board for England and Wales.

1   Adolescent Offending Profiles

Box 1.1 is an example of a common trajectory of engaging in thrill seeking or boredom relieving behavior during early adolescence and the behavior then escalates during mid-adolescence. Any identifiable offenses have been removed.

BOX 1.1 STUDY B SUBSAMPLE: A TYPICAL CASE STUDY ILLUSTRATING THE ESCALATION OF VIOLENCE

Co-arrests: First arrested for a public order offence in early adolescence for throwing stones at a derelict building. By the age of 15 behavior escalates. Arrests might include theft of a motor vehicle, theft, robbery at a shop, and burglary. Between the ages of 16 and 18 a charge for possession with intent to supply class A drugs out of area, robberies, and wounding.

Co-offenders: Generally, co-arrestees are same age or one or two years younger. For the out-of-area drug offenses, co-offenders are typically between 10 and 30 years older.

Solo arrests: Early solo arrests often coincide with the escalation of co-offending in early adolescence. Offenses included criminal damage, possession of cannabis, violent reactions when challenged by authorities or parents or when in care assault of care workers. These are reactive responses when there is a threat of punishment or perceived disrespect. Physical attacks can be particularly violent.

Understanding the range of offenses, the young person's role, and motivations is essential to supporting them. In the case study in Box 1.1 aggressive solo offenses are generally reactive and related to personal use of cannabis. The acquisitive crimes and involvement with drug trafficking involved

DOI: 10.4324/9781003255697-2

other people. However, when in a group he became the main aggressor. This transition from expressive or reactive aggression to instrumental violence is common as adolescents age and presents a rationale for supporting young people who exhibit signs of reactive anger and aggression in the early stages. Early aggressive behaviors can often be a response to other life factors. Therefore, focusing on the behavior alone is unlikely to support the young person comprehensively, nor will it prevent future aggression.

Understanding Behaviors

The official record offers an insight into the life experiences of adolescents from Study B and helps to contextualize the impact of familial and generational risk on a young person's behavior and future outlook. What follows is a typical example. Both parents suffer from substance addition and acute mental illness. Between 20 and 30 domestic violence incidents perpetrated by the father. Because of this, the young person is placed in a care home for extended periods of his childhood. A diagnosis of ADHD with the young person not wishing to take medications; a common occurrence for young people who suffer from this disorder because of the side effects of the drugs used for treatment. The young person becomes a regular user of cannabis and cocaine before the age of 15. Early offenses are likely a result of childhood trauma, learned behavior, low parental supervision, and were exacerbated the untreated diagnosis of ADHD. The acquisitive co-offences by the age of 16 include drug selling with a family member and progress to involvement with an organized drug selling operation out of area (so-called county lines).

Parental risks included a father with 20 to 40 convictions, including violent and acquisitive crimes, and a mother with arrests for reactive violence. Both parents and any older siblings had significant records of victimization were classified as vulnerable adults. As the young person approaches late adolescence the records indicate violence and extortion on behalf of a criminal gang and an arrest for a child protection offense, demonstrating the shift from exploited to instigator. This is a composite example to illustrate the cycle of violence and victimization for many of the young people in Study B subsample. It shows the importance of identifying at risk children as early as possible both for their own protection and life prospects, and for other vulnerable young people.

Differentiating Crimes

Typically, crime is reported according to legal classifications and seriousness. This approach leaves those supervising young people with the task of understanding how to effectively support them according to the presence of certain criteria. For example, whether key risks are present (e.g., violence, drug use, gang membership) and whether there are violent components to offending behavior. However, legal categorizations do not take account of the psychological explanations for a particular act or indeed series of offenses (Youngs, 2006; Canter & Youngs, 2009). This is especially true for types of violent offending. Feshbach classified two types of aggression: "A distinction is made between expressive aggression and hostile aggression which is illustrated in the difference between the desire to hit and the desire to hurt" (Feshbach, 1964, p. 270). A single category of offense could be the result of either. For example, criminal damage (a property crime) and assault (a person focused act) can be the result of a loss of control or learned reactive response. Equally, an offender may be in control and use violence to intimidate or as an act of planned revenge. Single categories of offense have successfully been distinguished by psychologists. Canter and Fritzon's (1998) paper on differentiating arsonists demonstrated that there were expressive and instrumental acts of arson, which could be further divided into person- or object-focused events. Three of these were represented in the offending behaviors of samples represented in the current publication (Table 1.1). Each of the motivations for arson cited in the examples requires different kinds of behavioral interventions. Burning down the abandoned building was for fun and to assert the group's collective commitment to breaking social and legal boundaries. The young person who described having a fire-starting kit mentioned this in passing and said that it made him

Table 1.1 Categories of arson with examples from the studies

Modes of arson[a]	Features	Example[b]
Instrumental object	Opportunistic fire setting	Burning down an abandoned house which was identified when the offender was smoking cannabis with friends
Expressive object	Often serial fire setting for emotional relief	A young person who had a fire-starting kit (metal box, matches, expedient) for use in his bedroom
Instrumental person	Triggered response to a targeted person, such as revenge	A young person who attempted to start a fire at a shop where he had been racially abusing the owner
Expressive person	Internally directed, seeking attention from family or authorities	A young person who threatened to set fire to himself and the family home after an argument with his mother.

[a]According to Canter and Fritzon, 1998.
[b]Examples from the data for the present publication.

feel calm when he lit the fires. In this sense it was therapeutic and something that he engaged in alone. The revenge offense represented an escalation of harassment and was a response to the victim reporting the offender's behavior to the authorities. Finally, the young person who threatened to set fire to himself and the family home following an argument; the report suggests wanting to cause emotional distress or to obtain a response. This last category is less common than the first three modes (Canter & Fritzon, 1998); this was also true for the three cohorts studied for the present publication.

Offending Stages

It is extremely unusual for a young person to move immediately to involvement with violent and organized crime without exhibiting any previous offending behaviors. From all three studies there was one example cited by a 17-year-old who reported being asked by a stranger if he wanted to make some additional money and who became involved in a daily routine of going out his area to a town about two hours away to sell cocaine and heroin (Box 7.2). His only other self-reported offense was fighting, nor did he have friends who offended. He was, however, in an area known to sell counterfeit items when he was approached, showing the dangers for young people who encounter older criminals.

Early police contact for the total sample for Study B revealed that young people were initially arrested for minor theft (including shoplifting), affray, assault, and criminal damage (Ashton et al., 2021). So, a mixture of non-violent income-generating and expressive violent behaviors. The next stage for some young people then included the use of aggressive tactics for purpose, such as possession of an offensive weapon, putting people in fear, racially aggravated offenses, and robbery (other than armed). However, the researchers found that burglary, which is typically deemed less serious, was found to be an early indication for later involvement with organized crime.

The arrests for the Study B subsample offenders followed a similar pattern to the entire group (Ashton et al., 2021). Three regions were found in the smallest space analysis, and they also represent the broader stages of arrests on timelines (Figure 1.1). The right region contains expressive violent crimes against property and people. Assault was also the most common offense, with 91% of the sample arrested for this offense alone (68% with others). Close to these violent offenses is possession of a class B controlled drug, typically cannabis from the records. All three crimes are common on the early arrest records for adolescents and effectively represent stage 1 on the offending timelines for some young people. Key points to consider here for professionals who are supporting young people: (1) Whether the young person is acting alone or with others; (2) If they show aggressive behaviors

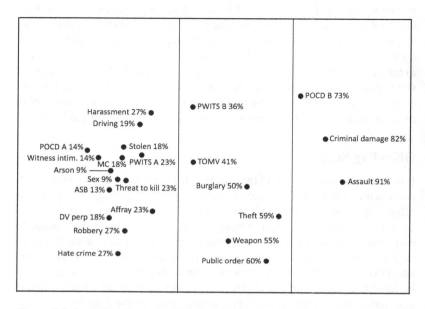

Figure 1.1 Study B subsample: SSA showing the relationship between solo arrests Coefficient of alienation = 0.12. Percentages represent solo arrests (for co-arrests see Figure 1.5).

Key: DV perp = domestic violence perpetrator; ASB = antisocial behavior; Stolen = used a stolen card; MC = malicious communications; TOMV = theft of a motor vehicle; POCD = possession of a controlled drug (A or B); PWITS = possession with intent to supply class A or B drugs.

solely for expressive or reactive reasons or is there an element of instrumental gain. (3) What the underlying causes of the behavior might be (home, school, peer group); (4) Why are they using cannabis, how often, and where are they acquiring it. Table 1.2 illustrates initial and subsequent behavioral stages, common responses to these points with suggested points of action or consideration.

The points in Table 1.2 help to identify the different levels of risk presented by the behaviors at this early stage. It is also worth noting that some young people may start at phase one but then progress to a second stage; thus, these points require monitoring. The offenses in the central region of Figure 1.1 represent a second stage and escalation of behaviors. These are predominantly income-generating (burglary, theft, possession with intent to supply class B drugs) with a continuation of an expressive behavior (public order). Theft of a motor vehicle can start as a thrill-seeking activity but develop into an income- or social status–generating crime (Chapter 6).

Table 1.2 Assessment considerations for early adolescent behavioral problems

Point	Phase/Stage 1	Phase/Stage 2
1	With others – consider peer influence or criminal exploitation	Alone – consider underlying causes (see point 3) and psychological well-being
2	Expressive – psychological assessment, consider ADHD, BESD and trauma response (see point 3)	Instrumental –consider peer influence, criminal exploitation, escalation of behavior to instigator
3	Familial cause – comprehensive assessment and support including the whole family	External cause – consider managing peer contact, other pro-social activities. Behavioral plan in place for school with individual support
4	Socially with others at weekends and provided by others – peer influence and dangers of substance use	Alone, during the week, purchasing themselves or acquiring from family or older friends – exploitation risk

Weapon carrying is also in this region, and just over half of the sample of 22 young adults had been arrested for this offense (Chapter 4).

The final region on the SSA plot (Figure 1.1) represents an escalation of income-generating behaviors (robbery, possession with intent to supply class A drugs, handling stolen goods,), instrumental violence (witness intimidation, threat to kill), and expressive aggression (DV perpetrator, hate crime, antisocial behavior). The records indicated that some behaviors can be expressive or instrumental (malicious communications, harassment, arson, affray, sexual assault, driving offenses). Finally, possession of a class A drug represents a change in drug use, possibly associates, and an increased risk of involvement with organized criminal groups through drug debt and purchasing.

Another way of considering the relationship between offenses is illustrated by self-reported data from Study A, involving young people who were three to five years behind those in Study B (Figure 1.2). Here the SSA plot can be divided into different stages and motivations. The offenses listed in stages 1 and 2 are the more common self-reported behaviors and represent two distinct initial pathways to involvement in violent income-generating offenses. Some young people in this sample demonstrate a combination of the two categories of offenses, which is why they appear in the same region on the left of the plot. The next stage is thrill-seeking behaviors; this is also situated in the upper region of the plot, next to expressive violence, because there are overlaps between the two. Finally instrumental violence and income-generating crimes, including robbery, burglary, carjacking, and

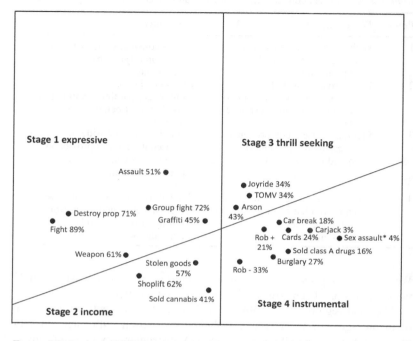

Figure 1.2 Study A: SSA showing the stages of self-reported offending
Coefficient of alienation = 0.10.

Key: TOMV = theft of a motor vehicle; Robbery with (+) and without (-) a weapon;
cards = use of stolen cards; *sexual offenses were from the police arrest records.

selling class A drugs, are clustered together. These crimes suggest a degree
of criminal training and confidence. Sexual assault was taken from the official record and was also found in this region. These data can also be viewed
in terms of risk. Expressive offenses demonstrate a lack of self-control,
group influences, and weapon carrying. Income-generating crimes can be
related to the need to make money. Thrill-seeking behaviors again show a
lack of control and the risk of being identified by older criminals because of
the ability to steal motor vehicles. The instrumental region is suggestive of
criminal grooming and exploitation by older or more experienced offenders.
Although these stages are present on referral and assessment forms, they are
not explicitly recorded, and it can be difficult to make an informed assessment from the official record summaries. This observation is exacerbated by
the length of some of these records, which can be up to 200 pages in some
instances.

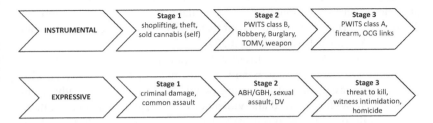

Figure 1.3 Study B: Stages of expressive and instrumental violence in the arrest data

When the order of offenses in the arrest records for Study B (both samples) were considered there were a combination of expressive and income-generating offenses that emerged in a particular order (Figure 1.3). This reflected the relationship between offenses that are highlighted in Figures 1.1 and 1.2; however, a useful difference was the appearance of robbery and burglary on offending timelines before young people became embedded in organized criminal gangs (Ashton et al., 2021). In this respect, these two categories of offending flag the need for a comprehensive and targeted prevention program to be implemented. They indicate that a young person is being exploited criminally and at risk of further exposure to adult criminal manipulation. Their importance as indicators of criminal exploitation will be discussed further in Chapter 6.

Relational Framework for Adolescent Samples

As noted, Canter and Youngs (2009, p. 99, fig. 5.3) reported the limitation of legal framework for understanding offending and highlighted the need to consider the co-occurrence of actions in their model of "variation between crimes". The result was a "spectrum" of offenses showing the overlap between (1) property-focused crimes (motoring, burglary, theft, robbery); (2) person-focused offenses (robbery, murder, violence, rape); (3) internal crimes (arson, drugs, motoring). The authors also stress the importance of building a framework of crimes that are specific to sets of data. Incentives also play an important role in our understanding of criminal behavior. This builds on early work by Youngs (2006) on what she terms "fundamental incentives", by expounding tenets of Bundura's Social Cognitive Theory (1986). This recognizes the importance of self-belief in thought, motivation, and actions, and posits that self-efficacy is nurtured through positive social reinforcement. Youngs identified three out of Bandura's seven incentives and explained the motivation for crimes in her sample: power and status; sensory (excitement and stimulation); and material incentives. There are overlaps between these motivations if we consider the data from Study C (Ashton & Bussu, 2020, 2022).

The framework for the current publication is based on the stages of offending in Studies A and B and is illustrated in Figure 1.4 (see also stages in Figure 1.3). Not all young people follow the same pathway to involvement with organized and violent crime (Chapter 7). However, there are typically overlaps between early expressive aggression, thrill-seeking behaviors, nonviolent income-generating, and a progression to instrumental violence.

Table 1.3 shows the most common arrests for the Study B sample of prolific offenders, plus possession with intent to supply class A drugs (in reference to organized crime exposure). A higher percentage of the sample were arrested for income-generating offences in the presence of others, demonstrating the importance of group membership. In most cases the co-offenders were different for each arrest, illustrating the relevance of wider criminal networks beyond gangs. Where this subsample differs from the entire sample (Ashton et al., 2021) is in the carrying/use of weapons.

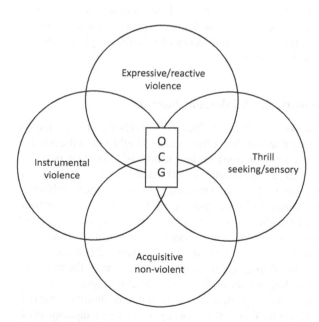

Figure 1.4 Relationship between offense categories for adolescents

Table 1.3 Study B subsample: Number of common/key arrest offences and style

Category	Offence	Total arrests	N solo arrests	N co-arrests	Sample % Solo	Sample % Co
Violence	Public order	93	66	27	55	60
Violence	Criminal damage	105	53	52	82	73
Violence	Assault	103	55	48	91	68
Violence	Knife/weapon	58	18	40	50	72
Income	PWITS class A	30	10	20	23	50
Income	Theft	87	34	53	59	77
Income	TOMV	133	26	107	41	68
Income	Burglary	97	20	77	50	82
Violence/Income	Robbery	47	8	39	27	68

The entire sample was more likely to carry a weapon alone, a finding that accords with the academic literature on weapons carrying (Oudekerk & Morgan, 2016). However, a higher percentage of the sample of 22 offenders were arrested with a weapon in the company of others. The case studies indicated that this group of young people used weapons instrumentally to obtain money or items, offenses that were generally committed in the company of others. The figures also reveal the development of more autonomous instrumental offending for the cohort, which is typical for late adolescents and young adults as they mature, gain skills, and become more confident in their offending (Moffitt, 1993).

Offending Styles

Another indicator of the degree of behavioral risk that a young person presents is their style of offending both during adolescence (Ashton et al., 2020; Goldweber et al., 2011) and into adulthood (Moffit, 1993). An offense can be committed either alone (solo), with one or more people as part of a temporary co-offending pair or group, or by a more established group as part of that collective identity. This may seem obvious, but it is something that is often neglected when planning behavioral programs. An intervention for someone who only offends in the company of other people would need to include support for resisting peer influence and recognizing exploitation. Determining offending style from official records is not as straightforward as it might first appear. Offenses can involve someone at the planning stages who is absent during the commissioning of a crime. A classic example of this might be a more experienced adult offender's role in planning a burglary with young people (Lantz & Ruback, 2017). He (typically) may instruct young people, drop them off at the location, and then leave the scene until he knows that the crime plan was completed successfully and without attention. This type of relationship is often difficult to determine from arrest data alone because the instigator and/or recruiter are absent. Additionally young people often hesitant to reveal the identities of their co-offenders either because they are too scared to do so or because they have been schooled in a "code" of criminal conduct (not naming others).

Offending style has long been recognized as an indicator for persistent and prolific offending (McCord & Conway, 2002; Moffitt, 1993; Reiss, 1988; Zimring, 1981). Traditionally young people are understood to initially to co-offend, with some gaining autonomy and continuing their criminal careers into adulthood (Reiss & Farrington, 1991). More recently studies using police data in Canada (Andresen & Felson, 2010, 2012), England (Ashton et al., 2021), and the United States (Stolzenberg & D'Alessio, 2016) have demonstrated that solo offending for some young people is more common and occurs at an earlier age than previously thought. Analyses of data from the US Pathways to Desistance Study (Ashton et al., 2020; Goldweber et al., 2011) have shown that young people who commit offenses alone and with others during the same period (so-called contemporaneous mixed-style offenders). This group commits significantly more crimes than adolescents who are exclusively solo or co-offenders. Furthermore, these self-reported data indicated that gang members reported mixed-style offending at an earlier age than young people who were criminally involved but not gang-affiliated.

Over 88% of the Study A cohort reported mixed-style total offending, and 87% stated that they committed violent crimes against property (damage to property, arson) and the person (fighting, weapon carrying, carjacking, assault) alone and with others during the same period (Tables 1.3 and 1.4). Contrary to traditional adolescent trajectories a minority of 5% of the young people reported only committing violence with others. This can perhaps be explained by the sample, who were participants in a program for gang and violent offending. The number of individuals who acted violently exclusively alone was also low at 8%. Their offenses related to a lack of impulse control and were reactive or expressive. The large number of mixed style violent offenders represents the instrumentalization of aggression and violence. An example of this would be a young person who responds impulsively and aggressively to a situation when alone and who becomes the main instigator of violence when in a group. The case study summary at the start of this chapter (Box 1.1) illustrates such a shift and demonstrates how

Table 1.4 Study A: Self-reported offending style

Category and style SRO	N	%
Income		
Solo	8	10.3
Co	19	24.4
Mixed	51	65.4
Violent		
Solo	8	8.0
Co	5	5.0
Mixed	87	87.0
Delinquent		
Solo	8	11.9
Co	30	44.8
Mixed	29	43.3
Total		
Solo	8	7.8
Co	4	3.9
Mixed	91	88.3

early expressive behaviors can lead to an increase in violence in a group (Lantz & Kim, 2019). Robbery, an acquisitive crime with a violent element, was measured with and without use of a weapon for Study A. Robbery without a weapon was more common (29%) than robbery with (19%). The most reported style for robbery without a weapon was co-offending (53%), with an even number of 24% who offended alone or mixed their style. For robbery with a weapon 50% reported exclusively co-offending, 36% varied their style, and only 14% reported offending alone. For the total income-generating crimes (burglary, shoplifting, handling stolen goods, breaking into a car to steal, used a car illegally, drug selling, robbery) 65% of the sample reported mixed-style offending, 24% only offended with others, and 10% only ever acted alone. The higher percentage of exclusive co-offenders for acquisitive crimes compared to those using violence represents skill transfer. Some crimes also require access to a criminal network (drug selling, handling stolen goods) or training (burglary, shoplifting, breaking into a car).

Three crimes were associated with boredom relief or thrill seeking/sensory gain (graffiti, theft of a motor vehicle, joyriding). Although theft of motor vehicle is typically associated with joyriding, some of the young people in Study C progressed to organized vehicle theft after a history of stealing motorbikes and cars for fun (see Chapter 6). This category was divided with 45% exclusively co-offending and 43% mixed style. The minority of 12% reported only offending alone.

Establishing offending style is crucial for understanding the most effective way of supporting young people. The presence of solo and co-offending together on official records is a strong indicator of increased risk (Ashton et al., 2020; Hodgson & Costello, 2006) and could be used to identify and divert high-risk individuals early. If used as a vulnerability indicator, it is also less stigmatizing and subjective than the label of "gang involved" (Ashton et al., 2020). For adolescents expressive solo offending is more about a lack of impulse control and does not necessarily indicate autonomy. For income-generating offenses co-offending can represent a learning or skill transfer stage, followed by more self-sufficient stage.

Skill Transfer and Offending

Co-offending is not a single category, there are different classifications (Ashton & Bussu, 2022). These classes are age (older, peer, younger); permanence (temporary, family, friends, group with a criminal focus); motivation (income, fun, social status); involvement (instigator, recruiter, follower); engagement (willing, exploited, coerced); initiation planned

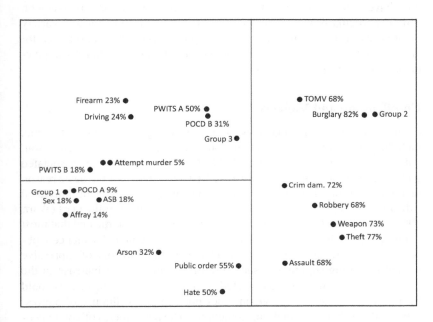

Figure 1.5 Study B subsample: The relationship between co-arrestee age and offense category

Coefficient of alienation = 0.11. Percentages represent the number of young people who committed the offense as a co-offender (for solo offending percentages see Figure 1.1). Group 1 = peers; Group 2 = 5 to 10 years older; Group 3 = co-offenders born from 1980s to 1960s.

(targeted, advantageous, consequential), or impulsive (opportunistic, impetuous, reactive). Some of these groupings are related. For example, an adolescent who offends with younger children is likely to fulfill the role of instigator or recruiter. These categories are not necessarily fixed either for individual offenses or for the stages of an adolescent offending timeline (Ashton et al., 2021). Uhnoo (2016) found that roles in the commissioning of arson are fluid and that an individual can fulfill multiple positions during the orchestration of a crime. She separated arson into two phases and identified a total of nine different roles for planning (motivator, strategist, person with experience, person with information relating to the opportunity, keeper of resources) and implantation (driver, lookout, fire-setter, audience). Other crime categories require their own specific roles and can, as noted above, be affected by whether the offence was planned or opportunistic (Ashton & Bussu, 2022). Over time, the young person who becomes an instigator may once have been a follower or have been coerced into criminal involvement. This is particularly true for those who have a higher number and variety of offenses on their timelines. Criminal groups offer the opportunity for knowledge transfer from a more experienced, often older, offender to juveniles (Van Mastrigt & Farrington, 2011).

Co-offending and Violence

Group offending is associated with specific categories of violent crime, including affray, arson with intent to endanger lives, and robbery (Hodgson, 2007; van Mastrigt & Farrington, 2009). Co-offending has been associated with an escalation violence (Conway & McCord, 2002) for the basic reason that a larger group is more likely to include at least one violent individual (McGloin & Piquero, 2010) and on account of the social influences (Warr, 2002). The arrest data from Study B (both samples) also indicated that most young people who are involved in the use of instrumental violence (robbery, carjacking, aggravated burglary) have an initial history of expressive violent offending (fighting, assault, criminal damage). An increase in the use of violence is therefore associated with responsive violence. This could be an offense response if a victim does not comply or the use of aggression for the purpose of obtaining something. The percentages of young people in Study B subsample arrested income generating crimes with others were much higher than the number for solo offenses (Table 1.4). The same was true of knife carrying, although more detailed research indicated that weapons were associated with income-generating crimes. In contrast 91% of the sample had been arrested for a solo assault compared to 68% as a co-offender. Violence for this group of prolific arrestees was committed alone and in the company of others. However, when a third category of mixed-style offending is noted (Table 1.3) it is clear that larger numbers of young people who self-reported their behavioral style were able to offend alone for violent and income-generating offenses.

The Roles and Emotions of Offending

Offending desistance represents the cessation from criminal activity, and it remains the overall goal of offending behavioral programs and supervision. Researchers have argued that there are two stages to desistance (Maruna & Farrell, 2004; Maruna et al., 2004): primary desistance, which is the initial break from criminal involvement; and secondary desistance, which is sustained and coincides with an identity shift to former or non-offender. This change is apparent in the narratives of former offenders as they begin to view themselves in a new role (King, 2013), and it has been argued that this shared and self-reflection strengthens the identity change. Offending narratives are a relevant, but neglected, element in the management of young people who offend, even though they can play a crucial role for the implementation of appropriate offending behavioral programs.

The criminal narratives approach (Canter, 1994; Canter & Youngs, 2009) advocates that criminal behavior can only be understood within a framework of personal stories. What Canter (1994) terms "inner narratives" are particularly important for understanding the context of violent offending. This is because life narratives draw from childhood and adolescent behaviors as young people establish their identities and can become "distorted" and transfer to later life and behaviors (Canter 1994; McAdams, 1988). Since Canter (1994) first established the value of this approach there have been several studies (see for example Ioannou et al., 2015; Youngs & Canter, 2009, 2013) to explore offender narratives. Two studies have looked specifically at the narratives of young people (Ioannou et al., 2018) including co-offending (Ashton et al., forthcoming), showing the approach to be effective for young people who offend alone and with others. The method involves an interview with a participant describing the preparation, orchestration, and events after they committed a crime. They are then asked to complete two questionnaires relating to the narrative offense to explore how they interpret their actions and to understand their emotions. For adolescents Ioannou and colleagues (2018) identified three themes, combining the distressed revenger with depressed victim. For the young people in Study C four traditional themes were identified (Ashton et al., forthcoming). The following examples were identified based on the questionnaire and coding of the narrative.

BOX 1.2 STUDY C: ELATED HERO

Before I was just at mine, like just chilling. Then one of my mates rung me I was like, "What you doing?" and that so I told him what I'm doing and he was like, "Coming out for a bit, we've got a car," so I was like, "Yeah," and we went up to either [place 1] or [place 2].... We were just like driving about, obviously I was ringing people and that to see what everyone's doing, then we went to a garage 'cause me mate got hungry, so he was like he has to shop for that thing you make, Pot Noodle, so they made him a Pot Noodle, then we bought all drinks and that and we all got back in the car and we noticed the police so we drove off as normal, then we got round the corner we sped off and there was an undercover BM[W] and I think there was a Merc[ades] chasing us there, then we thought we lost 'em at these little barrier things 'cause we just drove right through.

We're all just like going all left and then trying to lose 'em, like the helicopter was behind us so we ditched the car and ran through some passageway, and we got to the end their mates, like three vans just pulled up at the side. So, we jumped over bins and hop in, then there was police dogs in back gardens and that so I was like, 'Nah fuck it, no chance, I'm stopping without being bit off one. (Ashton & Bussu, 2020; Ashton & Bussu, 2022; Ashton et al., forthcoming)

At the core of this narrative are the emotions of excitement and enthusiasm both in engaging with others during the offense and in the description of the subsequent police chase and escape from the police dogs. The role was fun, exciting, unstoppable, and an adventure (Ashton et al., forthcoming). The inclusion of more basic needs such as stopping off at the petrol station to obtain food and drinks suggests that this type of activity is familiar. The offenders were thinking of their basic needs, even though they were on an adventure. The young person reported that he stole cars to get the police to chase him when he was bored and because it was "fun". When asked how the incident had affected him, he responded by saying, "I just weren't bothered … I went in the cell and went to sleep". Relieving boredom is recognized as a motivation of adolescent offending (Warr, 2002); in this case the behavior was part of the participant's weekly routine. The young person in the case study was 16 years old. Other offenses included robbery with a weapon, sold cannabis, sold class A drugs, stole a car, stole money, shoplifted, fighting, assault, criminal damage, daily use of cannabis, use of cocaine at weekends.

BOX 1.3 STUDY C: CALM PROFESSIONAL

So, we snuck behind him and put the weapon through his head. Snuck behind his car, he was sat there smoking a joint. This guy was bangers anyway, he weren't a legit guy so we knew he wouldn't grass, innit. So, we snuck behind his car and put the thing to his head and said, 'Listen mate, take your hands off the wheel,' now I jumped in the back and put a knife to his neck and told him to get in the passenger. So we got him in the passenger, me mate jumped in the driver's seat and hands me the weapon in the back, so I've got the weapon put behind to the passenger and then we drove off, took him, dropped him off somewhere where he didn't know, kicked him out of his car and drove off in his car and left him there and took his phone off him so he couldn't call anyone and drove off in his car and then sold his car and bought another car and that was it. (Ashton & Bussu, 2020; Ashton & Bussu, 2022; Ashton et al., forthcoming)

The calm professional narrative role was that of a proficient offender, doing a job, in control, going to plan, powerful, knowing the risk, and wanting recognition. The associated emotions were feeling confident, clam, courageous, and thoughtful. Although this was a co-offense, the pair worked intuitively and in unison (Ashton et al., forthcoming). This offense was opportunistic and occurred when the friends were out looking for potential victims to rob (Ashton & Bussu, 2022). Toward the end of sharing his narrative the young person said that rather than formerly planning robberies he simply thought them through in his head and then committed them. This process further supports the allocated theme. The young person was 16 years old. Other offenses included robbery with a weapon, used a card illegally, sold cannabis, sold class A drugs, shoplifted, handled stolen goods, fighting, assault, arson, driven under the influence of drugs, carried a weapon, criminal damage, daily use of cannabis, and use of cocaine at weekends.

BOX 1.4 STUDY C: DISTRESSED REVENGER

Me and my mate was out about 9-10 o'clock on a Saturday and you get drunk people and this man was starting on my mate so I ran at him and pushed him saying "what you doing?" and he tried smashing a glass bottle of my head so I smacked him in the face and me and my mate started kicking and punching him while he was down just to protect ourselves from a glass bottle. Like, so then after that I got dragged away by my uncle's mate and my uncle's mate was having a word with me. I think he said "why did you do that?" and I went "did you see what he was going to do to my mate? He was going to smash a glass bottle over me and my mate and obviously I've got to protect my mate as he was like my brother at the time so, he was like a brother from another mother, we use to back each other, if I was in trouble he would come and if he was in trouble I would come and help. So when that was happening I had the adrenaline and I couldn't stop because I had blacked out and the only thing I remember was someone picking him up and asking if he was alright. (Ashton & Bussu, 2020; Ashton & Bussu, 2022; Ashton et al., forthcoming)

This theme combines the emotions of anger, worry, upset, sadness, and scared with manliness and the roles of revenge and compulsion (Ashton et al., forthcoming). Acting on behalf of his friend and in response to a threat from a "drunk". He explains his actions as a justifiable response to avert the harm his friend, and throughout the incident he is clear to state that his actions were out of concern for others and to protect them. The young person was 16 years old. Other offenses include robbery without a weapon, entered a building to steal, stole money, shoplifted, fighting, assault, destroyed property, and carried a weapon.

BOX 1.5 STUDY C: DEPRESSED VICTIM

Basically, I was on my way home from school, got home, got changed, sat in the living room, on the PlayStation, it was a standard day – I kept on getting phone calls – I just kept on blanking them thinking why am I getting rang this much? And then I answered one of the phone calls, and it was one of, like, my old mates, who I'm not in association with no more, and he was like, "We're all on our way to yours" – I was like, "Why, what's wrong? Has something happened?" and he was like, "We need go – we need to go to – we need go and have this fight, we're having it out with" – 'cause Area 1 and Area 2, do you know what I mean, the two boroughs are at each other's throats. So I was like, "Well, I'm not getting involved in it" – I went, "I'm busy" – he was like, "You need to come" – I went, "Why?" – he was like, "You need to back your boys" – so I was like, "I'll come, but I'm not doing nothing. Don't expect me to do nothing." Turned up there, I thought it was just going to be like a little – about ten people, you know what I mean. Turn up there, it was – my head fell completely off, 'cause it was about fifty-odd people. I was like, it's not a gang fight, this, it's a pissing battle, this, it's like, armour, and they had knives, stuff like that, and it all – I was like that, looking round me thinking "Is it necessary to have, like, blades, bats and everything, it's not necessary – use your fists if you're having a fight with someone" – and I didn't getting involved in none of the fighting, I was just there, but the police turned up, and I spotted the police, and as soon as I spotted the police I was like, "I'm off – I'm not getting involved in this" – got on – some kid who I knew who was sat there on his bike, I went "Getting on the back of your bike now, we're going" – kid was like, "Why?" – I was like, "Police" – and everyone turned round and spotted police, everyone – even like, both different sides, say, like Area 1 and Area 2, they just scattered like insects, basically, all

> different directions and the police, like, were chasing them and I was off out of it, but it was just the way as soon as everyone spotted the police, they stopped fighting and they just ran, and that was probably the worst, like, thing I've been involved in which has been not me.

Although initially this narrative appears to be closely related that of distressed revenger, it combines the emotions of irritation, confusion, and unhappiness with the roles of helplessness, manly, confused, being the only choice, and wanting to get it over with (Ashton & Bussu, 2022; Ashton et al., forthcoming). This is illustrated by the description of the lead up to the gang fight, when the young person is at home and tries to ignore the requests to support his friends. Later in his interview he complains about the use of weapons in fights and reflected that he was no longer interested in being involved in such activities. The young person was 16 years old. Other offenses included assault, robbery with weapon, carried a weapon, firearm, sold cannabis and class A drugs, criminal damage, arson, fighting, daily use of cannabis, and use of cocaine at weekends.

This method is a helpful way of understanding how young people experience the act of offending. It is also clear that the different themes require different support. Those who seek adventure may need an alternative activity to desist from illegal risk-taking behaviors. For those young people who see crime as an occupation, finding an acceptable legitimate alternative and focusing on their future careers may offer a strong incentive to redirect their behavior. The narratives of those who fit within the Depressed Victim and Distressed Revenger themes have a lack of responsibility in common. This aspect differentiates them and requires a particular focus for any planned behavioral intervention. There are other aspects of offending that command attention when supporting young people who offend. These are offending styles (solo, co, or mixed-style offender) which relate to their position within a group as an instigator, recruiter, or follower. Coercion and child criminal exploitation (CCE) are also increasingly common for income-generating crimes and can involve an additional risk of gang membership or involvement with organized crime groups (OCG).

Summary and Implications for Practice

Rather than classifying an offense by a legal definition in isolation it is essential to consider a psychological approach, motivation, and other offenses to fully understand behaviors. A single category of crime can have multiple motivations. Furthermore, the role that a young person plays in the orchestration of an offense can depend on motivation, their position within a group, and their attitudes to offending. Young people can offend exclusively alone, with others, or combine the two styles of offending during the same period. So-called contemporaneous mixed-style offenders commit significantly more offenses than those who limit themselves to one style. This category is also a better indicator of increased social and behavioral risk than gang membership in official data.

Three or four stages of offending were identified (Figures 1.1 and 1.2; Figure 1.3). These represent a progression to increased reactive aggression and the move from nonviolent income-generating crimes to instrumental violence. Burglary and robbery are key indicators of early exploitation and skill transfer by older offenders and represent a stage of exploitation before some young people progress to involvement in serious organized crime and the associated instrumental violence (Figure 1.5). They could therefore flag increased vulnerability for young people. The presence of adults who are five to ten years older than a young person (mid-adolescence) on arrest records is also an important early indication of criminal exploitation. Equally, those who are involved in organized criminal groups had co-arrestees who were over ten years older. Any adult co-offender on an arrest record should be considered an increased risk for criminal exploitation.

Interventions need to take account of the offending stage and style of a young person. They also need to consider the scope of all offenses rather than a single type of behavior. This is particularly important for young people who have low impulse control and who react violently to situations. Programs also need to consider whether the young person suffers from mental illness, take account of neurodiversity, and consider the impact of trauma and exposure to violence. The presence of substance use should be considered and treated at the same time as any psychological or behavioral interventions. Understanding a young person's "inner narrative" (Canter, 1995) of offending could be a helpful way to identify an appropriate program of support. This method focuses on how a young person views their involvement with crime rather than assuming that a particular offense is committed for a single motivation.

References

Andresen, M. A., & Felson, M. (2010). The impact of co-offending. *British Journal of Criminology*, *50*(1), 66–81.

Andresen, M. A., & Felson, M. (2012). Co-offending and the diversification of crime types. *International Journal of Offender Therapy and Comparative Criminology*, *56*(5), 811–829.

Ashton, S. A., & Bussu, A. (2020). Peer groups, street gangs and organised crime in the narratives of adolescent male offenders. *Journal of Criminal Psychology, 10*(4), 277–292.

Ashton, S.-A., & Bussu, A. (2022). The social dynamics of adolescent co-offending. *Youth Justice, 17*(3).

Ashton, S.-A., Ioannou, M., & Hammond, L. (forthcoming). Applying the criminal narrative roles and emotions to young people who offend in groups.

Ashton, S. A., Ioannou, M., Hammond, L., & Synnott, J. (2020). The relationship of offending style to psychological and social risk factors in a sample of adolescent males. *Journal of Investigative Psychology and Offender Profiling, 17*(2), 76–92.

Ashton, S. A., Valentine, M., & Chan, B. (2021). Differentiating categories of violent adolescent offending and the associated risks in police and youth offending service records. *International Journal of Offender Therapy and Comparative Criminology.*

Bundura, A. (1986). *Social foundations of thought and action: A social cognitive theory.* Prentice-Hall, Inc.

Canter, D. (1995). Psychology of offender profiling. In R. Bull & D. Carson (Eds.), *Handbook of psychology in legal contexts* (pp. 343–355). John Wiley & Sons Ltd.

Canter, D., & Fritzon, K. (1998). Differentiating arsonists: A model of firesetting actions and characteristics. *Legal and Criminological Psychology, 3*(1), 73–96.

Canter, D. V. (1994). *Criminal shadows: Inside the mind of the serial killer* (pp. 63–69). HarperCollins.

Canter, D. V., & Youngs, D. (2009). *Investigative psychology: Offender profiling and the analysis of criminal action.* John Wiley & Sons.

Feshbach, S. (1964). The function of aggression and the regulation of aggressive drive. *Psychological Review, 71*(4), 257–272.

Goldweber, A., Dmitrieva, J., Cauffman, E., Piquero, A. R., & Steinberg, L. (2011). The development of criminal style in adolescence and young adulthood: Separating the lemmings from the loners. *Journal of Youth and Adolescence, 40*(3), 332–346.

Hodgson, B. (2007). Co-offending in UK police recorded crime data. *The Police Journal, 80*(4), 333–353.

Hodgson, B., & Costello, A. (2006). The prognostic significance of burglary in company. *European Journal of Criminology, 3*(1), 115–119.

Ioannou, M., Canter, D., Youngs, D., & Synnott, J. (2015). Offenders' crime narratives across different types of crimes. *Journal of Forensic Psychology Practice, 15*(5), 383–400.

Ioannou, M., Synnott, J., Lowe, E., & Tzani-Pepelasi, C. (2018). Applying the criminal narrative experience framework to young offenders. *International Journal of Offender Therapy and Comparative Criminology, 62*(13), 4091–4107.

King, S. (2013). Early desistance narratives: A qualitative analysis of probationers' transitions towards desistance. *Punishment and Society, 15*(2), 147–165.

Lantz, B., & Ruback, R. B. (2017). A networked boost: Burglary co-offending and repeat victimization using a network approach. *Crime and Delinquency, 63*(9), 1066–1090.

Lantz, B., & Kim, J. (2019). Hate crimes hurt more, but so do co-offenders: Separating the influence of co-offending and bias on hate-motivated physical injury. *Criminal Justice and Behavior, 46*(3), 437–456.

Maruna, S., & Farrell, S. (2004). Desistance from crime: A theoretical reformulation. *Kolner Zeitschrift fur Soziologie und Sozialpsychologie, 43*, 171–194.

Maruna, S., Porter, L., & Carvalho, I. (2004). The Liverpool desistance study and probation practice: Opening the dialogue. *Probation Journal, 51*(3), 221–232.

McAdams, D. P. (1988). Biography, narrative, and lives: An introduction. *Journal of Personality, 56*(1), 1–18.

McCord, J., & Conway, K. P. (2002). Patterns of juvenile delinquency and co-offending. *Crime and Social Organization, 10*, 15–30.

McGloin, J. M., & Piquero, A. R. (2010). On the relationship between co-offending network redundancy and offending versatility. *Journal of Research in Crime and Delinquency, 47*(1), 63–90.

Moffitt, T. E. (1993). Adolescence-limited and life-course-persistent antisocial behavior: A developmental taxonomy. *Psychological Review, 100*(4), 674–701.

Oudekerk, B., & Morgan, R. E. (2016). *Co-offending among adolescents in violent victimizations, 2004–13.* US Department of Justice, Office of Justice Programs, Bureau of Justice Statistics.

Reiss Jr, A. J. (1988). Co-offending and criminal careers. *Crime and Justice, 10*, 117–170.

Reiss Jr, A. J., & Farrington, D. P. (1991). Advancing knowledge about co-offending: Results from a prospective longitudinal survey of London males. *Journal of Criminal Law and Criminology, 82*(2), 360–395.

Stolzenberg, L., & D'Alessio, S. J. (2016). A commentary on Zimring and Laqueur (2015): Juveniles and co-offending and why the conventional wisdom is often wrong. *Journal of Crime and Justice, 39*(4), 550–555.

Van Mastrigt, S. B., & Farrington, D. P. (2009). Co-offending, age, gender and crime type: Implications for criminal justice policy. *The British Journal of Criminology, 49*(4), 552–573.

Van Mastrigt, S. B., & Farrington, D. P. (2011). Prevalence and characteristics of co-offending recruiters. *Justice Quarterly, 28*(2), 325–359.

Warr, M. (2002). *Companions in crime: The social aspects of criminal conduct.* Cambridge University Press.

Youngs, D. (2006). How does crime pay? The differentiation of criminal specialisms by fundamental incentive. *Journal of Investigative Psychology and Offender Profiling, 3*(1), 1–19.

Youngs, D., & Canter, D. V. (2013). Offenders' crime narratives as revealed by the narrative roles questionnaire. *International Journal of Offender Therapy and Comparative Criminology, 57*(3), 289–311.

Zimring, F. E. (1981). Kids, groups and crime: Some implications of a well-known secret. *Journal of Criminal Law and Criminology, 72*(3), 867–885.

2 Substance Use and Drug Offenses

Case Studies

This chapter commences with two case studies featuring young people who, on paper at least, seem to have a similar relationship with drug use and sales. They are used here to illustrate the importance of considering each young person as an individual, with distinct needs. The second case study is a reminder that just as offending behaviors are dynamic, so is a young person's relationship with drugs. The case studies and research findings suggest that rather than thinking in terms of drug "prevention" and "interventions", it is essential to understand the unique relationship that an individual has with drugs. Sometimes these bonds are complex and always require a holistic and comprehensive response.

BOX 2.1 STUDY C: ATTITUDE TO CANNABIS SMOKING

Researcher: do you see carrying weed [cannabis] around and smoking it as a crime?

Participant: no not at all

Researcher: ok

Participant: It's not really a crime, is it?

Researcher: so, you wouldn't do anything to avoid getting caught?

Participant: no, I wouldn't, I mean I wouldn't smoke it in a very big place I mean everyone does it there that's why I was like oh ok it's fine, loads of skaters [people using skateboards] are smoking it do you know what I mean everyone's doing it, so I was like why can't I do it, you know what I mean, so I just rolled it up smoked it.

Researcher: What happened after you were arrested?

DOI: 10.4324/9781003255697-3

Participant: [it] lasted about half an hour I was just stood there for half an hour in cuffs people filming me and stuff like that I was like why you making me look like a proper criminal here. What you doing?

Researcher: How did you feel when you were standing there?

Participant: I don't know I was just like making jokes about it really, yeah I've got a brick just saying I've got like loads of weed somewhere stashed making their minds say different things just messing them up and that because there not catching I've not got anything to be caught with so I was taking the piss really but I'd never do that if I actually had something.

(16 years old, other offenses included fighting, selling cannabis, carried a weapon, daily cannabis use, occasional use of cocaine.)

The case study in Box 2.1 is an excerpt from an interview with a young person from Study C who had been arrested for smoking cannabis at a city center location on his way back from school. The other offenses that he self-reported were selling class A drugs, carrying a knife when he sold drugs, and fighting. In addition to using cannabis daily, he used cocaine at parties. He offended alone and with other people; this included selling cannabis with older friends. He was 16 at the time of the interview and lived mostly at home with his mother but spent time with his father and his grandparents. He believed that his father had a criminal record, but he did not know any details. His mother had never been involved in the justice system and had a full-time job, working as a professional.

BOX 2.2 STUDY B SUBSAMPLE: A REPRESENTATIVE EXAMPLE OF GENERATIONAL TRAUMA AND SUBSTANCE USE

A young person who grew up in a home with callouts for domestic violence from the age of two. By the age of 14 he was listed as missing from home and was criminally exploited by family members and men who were involved with organized crime. Both parents had convictions for violence and income-generating offenses, including possession and supply of class A and B drugs. While still a minor he was convicted with a family member for selling class A drugs. He had a diagnosis of ADHD, a learning disability, and was known to use cannabis from early adolescence and had access to class A drugs via his family. The familial problems with violence were generational. The young person was also known to be at risk from peer antisocial influence and was gang-affiliated; while still a minor he was arrested with much older co-offenders for stealing cars and was being exploited by an organized crime group selling class A drugs. His solo offenses related to drug selling and threats of violence. (Some details have been changed to protect the young person's identity.)

The two young people in the case studies were of the same age. The first young person self-reported a total of 9 offenses, and the second was arrested 26 times. Similarities between the two include involvement in the sale of class A drugs, older associates who were involved in drug selling, knife carrying, violent behaviors, and mixed-style offenders. The starkest difference between the two cases is the level of risk presented by the families of these young people. In this sense the family can present a risk or a protective factor (Hammersley, 2011). The young person in Box 2.2 suffered generational trauma and had been raised in a violent home. All adults in his immediate contact (including extended family) had a criminal record and were considered vulnerable adults. In contrast the young person who is cited in Box 2.1 came from a relatively stable family environment. Importantly there was at least one adult who had no criminal associates. These examples illustrate that the relationship between adolescents, substance use, and offending is not consistent or homogenous. Nor is this relationship fixed during adolescence. Young people with higher levels of adverse childhood experiences present an enhanced vulnerability of criminal exploitation by people outside of the family (Molina & Levell, 2020). This is recognized in the guidelines for supporting young people in the criminal justice system (YJB, 2022).

Adolescent Drug Use

When asked about their use of illegal substances, the young people who took part in Study A demonstrated considerable variance (ADIS; Moberg & Hahn, 1991). Even though 81% of the sample had used drugs, just over half were regular users at the time of starting an offending behavioral program (Table 2.1). Cannabis was the most used substance, with 73% having tried it and 51.3% reported using it on a regular basis. Around 11% were regularly using cocaine (typically at parties as described in case study 2.1). Small numbers of individuals had also tried "spice" (a synthetic cannabinoid), hallucinogens, amphetamines, downers, MDMA, prescription drugs (most commonly Xanax), other opiates, and steroids; one young person had tried heroin. When asked when they last used drugs, 54% reported they had used in the last week, and 35% had used them within 24 hours of the questionnaire. Alcohol was less of a problem for this cohort but was typically used by those who consumed drugs regularly. A young person from Study C explained that it was easier to purchase drugs than alcohol directly because a drug dealer would not require proof of age. Those who did drink regularly reported obtaining alcohol from older friends, a known method of criminal grooming (Mooney & Ost, 2013).

Just over half of the sample began using drugs between the ages of 10 and 13 years, four participants said that they started before the age of 10 years, and a further quarter said that they were between 14 and 15 years old when they first used substances (Table 2.2). Three different reasons for initiating

Table 2.1 Study A: Substance type and use

	N	%
Last drug use		
Never	21	18.8
Over a year	1	0.8
6–12 months	16	14.3
Several weeks	13	11.6
Last week	22	19.6
Yesterday	24	21.4
Today	15	13.4
Alcohol		
Never	37	43.5
Tried but quit	14	16.5
Several times a year	15	17.6
Several times a month	4	4.7
Weekends only	8	9.4
Several times a week	3	3.5
Several times a day	4	4.7
Cannabis		
Never	30	27.0
Tried but quit	15	13.5
Several times a year	1	0.9
Several times a month	8	7.2
Weekends only	3	2.7
Several times a week	30	27.0
Several times a day	24	21.6
Cocaine		
Never	82	73.9
Tried but quit	14	12.6
Several times a year	6	5.4
Several times a month	6	5.4
Weekends only	2	1.8
Several times a week	1	0.4

drug use were given. The majority of 49% reported that they like the feeling when they used drugs, 18% cited peer influence as the reason, and 33% were self-medicating. Not in the sense that they were seeking respite from their environment (Turner et al., 2018), but more literally because they felt that cannabis helped their mental illnesses or cognitive disorders such as ADHD. Young people who use drugs to relieve an illness also need support from specially trained mental health workers. Using drugs with peers requires an individual's relationship with their group to be reconsidered and assistance with resistance to peer influence. Comprehensively supporting the young person cited in Box 2.2 requires a more holistic approach. He represented half of this study sample; 50% of young people had family members who used drugs and 32% had a parent who had been arrested for drug dealing. Of this 32% the majority (86%) had convictions for selling class A drugs, suggesting either vulnerability as drug users or involvement with organized criminal groups. All the young people from this study had at least one parent with a criminal conviction for violence, and all had witnessed domestic violence as a child. Importantly in the context of the present publication, taking account of the impact of high levels of childhood adversity and substance use helps to explain his aggressive behavior from early adolescence.

Another important indicator when considering the risk that drug use presents is the time of day that someone first uses. Concerningly, 36% of Sample A reported using as soon as they wake up in the morning, or of waking up during the night. No significant relationship was found between using at these times and anxiety or depression as the reason for use. Therefore, the desire to smoke or take drugs at these times may suggest addiction, even though young people who reported high use of cannabis denied that they had an addiction. Consistent drug use requires targeted and professional intervention, not least of all because it can have a relationship to underlying trauma or addiction. Most general youth offending programs target young people who use because they like the feeling. However, the normalization of substance use within peer groups acts as a barrier to effective behavioral change (Parker et al., 2002). This is illustrated by 41% of the sample stating that there had been no negative impact of drug use on their lives. In contrast 26% reported having been arrested or punished for using drugs, and 20% had been in trouble at home. Programs may wish to consider discussing the impact of drug use with participants to determine whether it is the most effective way to support them. There should also be access to professional services for those who use drugs for trauma and mood disorders.

Although increasingly accepted socially and legal in some countries, regular cannabis use can impact academic performance, attention, and sleep (Ogeil et al., 2019; Tapert et al., 2002), which in turn can affect a young person's ability to engage in educational and social activities. Although not fully understood, chronic adolescent drug use is associated with long-term and irreversible changes to the brain (Camchong et al., 2017). This is because adolescence is a critical period for brain maturation and cognitive development (Fischer et al., 2020). The responses illustrated in Table 2.2 give further insight into vulnerability among adolescent drug use. The 53% of young people who reported using drugs with older friends are at risk of exploitation, and the 44% who cited using substances alone and/or to mask feelings of trauma, sadness, or anxiety need psychological assessment and support. It is essential to adopt a person-centered approach (Bosick, 2015; Tseng & Seidman, 2007), giving young people a voice and decision in how they can best be supported. However, it is impossible to ignore the scale and complexity of what justice involved young people face. Some of their

Table 2.2 Study A: Drug use

	N	%
Age at first use		
Never	14	13.2
Recently	2	1.9
After 15	4	3.8
14–15 years old	27	25.5
10–13 years old	55	51.9
Before the age of 10	4	3.8
Reason for use		
I like the feeling	44	49.4
To be like my friends	16	18.0
To feel like an adult	0	0
Nerves or worries	24	27.0
I feel sad/lonely	5	5.6
Typical time of use		
Night	30.2	30.2
Afternoon	19	22.1
Before or after school/work	10	11.6
When first wake up	16	18.6
Get up during the night	15	17.4
Use with		
Parents or relatives	3	3.4
Siblings	5	5.6
Peers	76	85.4
Older friends	47	52.8
Alone	39	43.8
Source of drugs		
Parties	16	17.2
Friends	55	59.1
Parents	1	1.1
Buy my own	59	63.4
Steal	1	1.1
Given by a dealer	1	1.1

experiences would be difficult for an adult to process without the support of psychological and therapeutic services. Relatively few academic papers ask young people directly about their lives. For the young people in the three studies included in the present publication, the reality of substance use poses a danger to their current (physical and psychological health, exploitation, drug debt) and future lives (adult criminal justice involvement). In the case study (Box 2.1) the young person's response to the question of whether he considered smoking cannabis to be illegal and his reaction to the arrest show he differentiated between the two acts of using and selling regarding illegality. He illustrated this further by going to locations that were away from the city center and security cameras when selling drugs to avoid detection. This case is supported by professional observations. A small survey of youth offending practitioners (Duke et al., 2020) found that professionals are aware that some young people see the use of cannabis as "normal" and unproblematic.

Differentiating between adolescent substance use and seeking to understand why a young person uses drugs is crucial for supporting them. Although youth justice professionals recognize the complex issues surrounding adolescent drug use (Duke et al., 2020), differentiating between the reasons why a young person uses rather than grading risk avoids labeling some young people as "problematic".

Drug Use and Crime

The above findings are supported internationally by research (Hammersley, 2011). Offenders are consistently more likely to report using illegal substances, although this observation does not necessarily represent a causal relationship. However, not all drug users engage in criminal behaviors (Hammersley et al., 1989). As Bean (2014, p. 39) points out, there are three possible explanations for the relationship between drug use and crime: drug use leads to crime, crime leads to drug use, or the two behaviors share a common cause. The answer has important implications for behavioral support programs. Although the substance use to crime model has the most support among criminologists (MacCoun et al., 2003), it is not supported by the cohorts who are represented in the studies for the present publication, largely because the model does not differentiate between the categories of crime or the different types of substances or indeed reasons for use. For example, Study B subsample (Figures 1.1 and 1.5) demonstrated that an arrest for possession of cannabis was associated with expressive violence, with 73% of the cohort having been arrested for possession alone and 31% with other people. Arrests for possession of a class A drug were far lower (14% of the sample alone and 9% with others) and were associated with increased violence and income-generating crimes. In the case of adolescents, drug use can be dynamic and can be impacted by social groups, trauma, and addiction.

Drug Use and Violence

Goldstein's (1985) model to explain the relationship between drugs and violence has three components: the psychopharmacological effects of substance use; the need to fund an illegal drug habit; and, finally, the occurrence of violent behaviors that are linked to the drug market. This last component forms the focus of the government's strategies toward violence; specifically, the involvement with organized crime and street gangs in the sale of drugs (HM Government, 2016, 2018). The relationship between substance abuse and serious violence is complex, because the two behaviors have many of the same risk factors (Hawkins et al., 1992; HM Government, 2018). Research suggests that heroin and other opiate use is also associated with acquisitive, but not violent, crimes (Hayhurst et al., 2017). Academic reviews indicate that cannabis has an indirect relationship with interpersonal violence, because early and long-term use impedes cognitive function, which in turn can impact an individual's ability to negotiate and respond to conflict (Moore & Stewart, 2005).

Substance use has been found to be a strong predictor of recidivism (Dowden & Brown, 2002) through the association of the user with marginalization and embeddedness with other users and drug subcultures (Schroeder et al., 2007). Research has also consistently indicated that substance use has a relationship to increased impulsivity (Feldstein Ewing et al., 2015). The same study also found that peers and family members who were involved in the justice system were associated with increased use of cannabis. One study on a sample of urban youth found a relationship between substance use and increased victimization (Pinchevsky et al., 2014). An increasing number of studies of UK samples have noted that drug debt can increase a young person's risk of criminal exploitation and involvement in drug selling and County Lines (Hesketh & Robinson, 2019).

Drug Selling

As with the case study in Box 2.1 some young people sell drugs to fund their own substance use. Young people in Study C reported obtaining cannabis from older siblings or friends and selling to peers who did not have easy access to the drug. The problem with this first stage of drug selling is that the adolescent selling drugs is vulnerable to further criminal exploitation. One of the young people from Study C reported how he had been identified by an adult who was involved in organized drug selling and he was then "tested" to see if he was able to prepare drugs for selling, a situation that he described as a kind of "job interview" (Ashton & Bussu, 2020; Ashton et al., forthcoming). When he had demonstrated that he could prepare drugs and sell them locally, he was then taken out of his area to prepare and sell drugs from a "trap house". He was only 16 years old at the time.

In Study A the young people self-reported class A drugs sales were associated with burglary, robbery, carjacking, and sexual assaults (Figure 1.2). Similarly arrests in Study B indicated that possession with intent to supply class A drugs was in the same region of the plot as expressive increased violence and activities that are associated with organized crime involvement (witness intimidation, threat to kill, robbery), and sexual assaults (Figure 1.1). The use of class A drugs before involvement in selling was also noted by Study C. This was partly because young people needed to fund their own increased drug use, but mostly because obtaining the drugs left them vulnerable to exploitation from the adult providers.

Summary and Implications for Interventions

Young people in Study A used drugs for different reasons: self-medicating, enjoyment, and with friends. Referral to professional services is necessary for those who use substances to cope with trauma or mood disorders. Programs could focus on supporting young people who use for social reasons or personal enjoyment. Since 45% of the sample could not cite any negative outcomes relating to drug use, interventions should focus on educating young people about the risks associated with regular substance use.

Figure 2.1 summarizes factors that could be used as a checklist to determine risk and category of intervention. Inquiring about the time of day, who a young person uses substances with, and which drugs they are exposed to can help support to be targeted. Young people move from using cannabis socially to being exposed to greater use or substance variety by older people. Using with older friends can also indicate criminal grooming and exploitation. Furthermore, secondary or class A drug use, any drug that is used to "self-medicate", any drug used in the mornings, or any drug used alone indicate higher risk. Young people will need access to mental health and trauma counseling for assessment and to support their drug interventions. Offending risk factors are also relevant here. The use of class A drugs also places young people at risk of criminal/sexual exploitation by adult criminals. Young people who suffer from comorbidity of substance use, exposure to violence, childhood trauma, and mental illness require comprehensive and holistic support. Asking a young person to decrease their level of substance use without supporting their mental illness is unlikely to work, and vice versa.

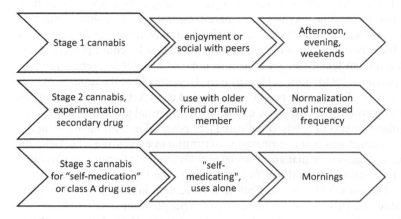

Figure 2.1 Key stages of substance use

References

Ashton, S. A., & Bussu, A. (2020). Peer groups, street gangs and organised crime in the narratives of adolescent male offenders. *Journal of Criminal Psychology*, *10*(4), 277–292.

Bean, P. (2014). *Drugs and crime*. Routledge.

Bosick, S. J. (2015). Crime and the transition to adulthood: A person-centered approach. *Crime and Delinquency*, *61*(7), 950–972.

Camchong, J., Lim, K. O., & Kumra, S. (2017). Adverse effects of cannabis on adolescent brain development: A longitudinal study. *Cerebral Cortex*, *27*(3), 1922–1930.

Dowden, C., & Brown, S. L. (2002). The role of substance abuse factors in predicting recidivism: A meta-analysis. *Psychology, Crime and Law*, *8*(3), 243–264.

Duke, K., Thom, B., & Gleeson, H. (2020). Framing 'drug prevention' for young people in contact with the criminal justice system in England: Views from practitioners in the field. *Journal of Youth Studies*, *23*(4), 511–529.

Feldstein Ewing, S. W., Filbey, F. M., Loughran, T. A., Chassin, L., & Piquero, A. R. (2015). Which matters most? Demographic, neuropsychological, personality, and situational factors in long-term marijuana and alcohol trajectories for justice-involved male youth. *Psychology of Addictive Behaviors*, *29*(3), 603–612.

Fischer, A. S., Tapert, S. F., Louie, D. L., Schatzberg, A. F., & Singh, M. K. (2020). Cannabis and the developing adolescent brain. *Current Treatment Options in Psychiatry*, *7*(2), 144–161.

Goldstein, P. J. (1985). The drugs/violence nexus: A tripartite conceptual framework. *Journal of Drug Issues*, *15*(4), 493–506.

Hammersley, R. (2011). Pathways through drugs and crime: Desistance, trauma and resilience. *Journal of Criminal Justice*, *39*(3), 268–272.

Hammersley, R., Forsyth, A., Morrison, V., & Davies, J. B. (1989). The relationship between crime and opioid use. *British Journal of Addiction*, *84*(9), 1029–1043.

Hayhurst, K. P., Pierce, M., Hickman, M., Seddon, T., Dunn, G., Keane, J., & Millar, T. (2017). Pathways through opiate use and offending: A systematic review. *International Journal of Drug Policy*, *39*, 1–13.

Hawkins, J. D., Catalano, R. F., & Miller, J. Y. (1992). Risk and protective factors for alcohol and other drug problems in adolescence and early adulthood: Implications for substance abuse prevention. *Psychological Bulletin*, *112*(1), 64.

Hesketh, R. F., & Robinson, G. (2019). Grafting: "the boyz" just doing business? Deviant entrepreneurship in street gangs. *Safer Communities*, *18*(2), 54–63.

HM Government. (2016). *Ending gang violence and exploitation*. Home Office.

HM Government. (2018). *Serious violence strategy*. Home Office.

MacCoun, R., Kilmer, B., & Reuter, P. (2003). Research on drugs-crime linkages: The next generation. In R. MacCoun, B. Kilmer & P. Reuter (Eds.), *Toward a drugs and crime research agenda for the 21st century* (pp. 65–95).

Moberg, D. P., & Hahn, L. (1991). The adolescent drug involvement scale. *Journal of Child and Adolescent Substance Abuse*, *2*(1), 75–88.

Molina, J., & Levell, J. (2020). Children's experience of domestic abuse and criminality: A literature review. *Published review of the Victims' Commissioner for England and Wales*, National Insitute of Justice.

Mooney, J.-L., & Ost, S. (2013). Group localised grooming: What is it and what challenges does it pose for society and law? *Child and Family Law Quarterly*, *25*(4), 1–20.

Moore, T. M., & Stuart, G. L. (2005). A review of the literature on marijuana and interpersonal violence. *Aggression and Violent Behavior*, *10*(2), 171–192.

Ogeil, R. P., Cheetham, A., Mooney, A., Allen, N. B., Schwartz, O., Byrne, M. L., Simmons, J. G., Whittle, S., & Lubman, D. I. (2019). Early adolescent drinking and cannabis use predicts later sleep-quality problems. *Psychology of Addictive Behaviors*, *33*(3), 266–273.

Parker, G. A., Royle, N. J., & Hartley, I. R. (2002). Intrafamilial conflict and parental investment: A synthesis. *Philosophical Transactions of the Royal Society of London. Series B: Biological Sciences*, *357*(1419), 295–307.

Pinchevsky, G. M., Fagan, A. A., & Wright, E. M. (2014). Victimization experiences and adolescent substance use: Does the type and degree of victimization matter? *Journal of Interpersonal Violence*, *29*(2), 299–319.

Schroeder, R. D., Giordano, P. C., & Cernkovich, S. A. (2007). Drug use and desistance processes. *Criminology*, *45*(1), 191–222.

Tapert, S. F., Baratta, M. V., Abrantes, A. M., & Brown, S. A. (2002). Attention dysfunction predicts substance involvement in community youths. *Journal of the American Academy of Child and Adolescent Psychiatry*, *41*(6), 680–686.

Tseng, V., & Seidman, E. (2007). A systems framework for understanding social settings. *American Journal of Community Psychology*, *39*(3), 217–228.

Turner, S., Mota, N., Bolton, J., & Sareen, J. (2018). Self-medication with alcohol or drugs for mood and anxiety disorders: A narrative review of the epidemiological literature. *Depression and Anxiety*, *35*(9), 851–860.

YJB. (2022). *AssetPlus outcome evaluation: Final report*. Youth Justice Board for England and Wales.

3 Expressive Violence

BOX 3.1 STUDY C: CASE STUDY OF ASSAULT

Yeah. So then they were just shouting stuff and from there we all just thought they can't be shouting anything so we all just attacked them. I made the decision. Everybody else was just a bit scared because the people outside the pubs were drunk and a bit older. But one of the girls was like my girlfriend at the time so I wasn't going to allow it so I just ran over at the start, threw a dig and then I got hit back and then all my mates just ran over and we all just done them in from there. It's just seeing red, isn't it really? I couldn't really explain how I felt, I just thought, I just looked around and then clenched my fists and my adrenaline just raised and raised and raised and I just thought it's got to be done. They can't be shouting that to kids. Because if it was my daughter someone was shouting that to about twenty years older, I'd go mad myself. So I just completely lost it and just seeing red and ran at them and just did what I did. Well at first I just threw one dig and then it hit one of them and then next I'm getting grabbed by about three of the people outside the pub and one of them is hitting me and that's just when all my mates ran over and just started laying into them all. And then it just like they all ended up on the floor so we all just ended up hitting them a few more times and then we had to run off from there because the police got called. (15 years old)

Box 3.1 recounts an incident from Study C when the young person was around 13 years old. He and a group of around 50 friends were walking through a shopping center at night and some of the men who were standing outside of a pub starting shouting to the young women who were a part of

DOI: 10.4324/9781003255697-4

his group. The offending narrative falls within the distressed revenger role (Ashton et al., forthcoming). There are other important points that help to explain why young people become involved in expressive violence during early adolescence. First, the young person describes his reaction to the name-calling. Second, although he couldn't explain how he felt, he was aware that his "adrenaline just raised and raised and raised" giving him the courage to act. The point here is that he did not describe losing control but rather waiting until he felt strong enough to react. When reflecting on the event he told the researcher that if the same thing happened three years after the incident he would probably just "laugh at someone". This indicates self-awareness of maturing and having more self-control. Third, the influence of the group; he stated that had he not responded to the name-calling then his friends might have laughed at him (Ashton & Bussu, 2020; Warr, 2002), thus showing peer group pressure. Fear of ridicule is a recognized risk among adolescent group members and is influenced by the need to avoid rejection (Kiesler & Kiesler, 1970; Warr, 2002). Finally, although the young person was with a large group of peers, he makes it clear that he reacted and initiated the assault. Points three and four illustrate the complexity of group influence. An individual can feel it necessary to react according to their role in a group and consequently lead others to be involved in violence. In this case the individual needed assistance when the stronger targets of his attack got the better of him.

Expressive Violent Crimes

Expressive violence is defined here as a reactive or emotional response to a stimulus against a person or property. These offenses typically appear early on a young person's behavioral timeline and are common (Box 3.1). In Study A, examples that were self-reported were assault, destroying property, and fighting (Figure 1.2). In Study B, assault and criminal damage appeared early on timelines and were typically aimed at peers (Box 1.1), which concurs with previous studies (Oudekerk & Morgan, 2016). As they aged toward late adolescence this cohort of young people were arrested for violence against their families, which emerged in the form of domestic violence (DV) and/or malicious communications. It is possible that DV occurred earlier but that it remained unreported because research has indicated that families often hesitate to involve the authorities when they are victims of physical abuse by their child (Condry & Miles, 2013). Malicious communication arrests were typically focused on current or former partners.

Other related offenses included affray (a public order offense causing someone to fear for their safety). This was less common in the arrest data from Study B but presents an equivalent to the self-reported fighting in

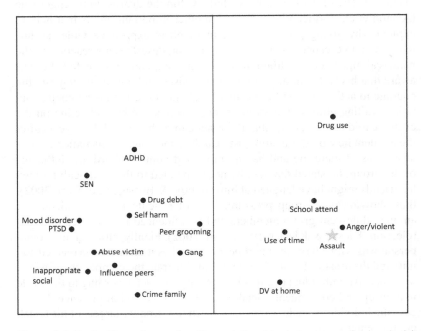

Figure 3.1 Study B total sample: The relationship between professional risk
assessment and assault

Coefficient of alienation = 0.08.

Study A. Similarly, an arrest for a section 4 public order offense (defined as
the use of threatening or abusive words or behavior) was also less common.
Table 3.1 shows the percentages of each sample to have reported or been
arrested for an expressive violent offense according to these categories. A
comparison between the total cohort and the top 22 offenders from Study B

Table 3.1 Expressive offending in studies A and B

Offense	Study A self-report	Study B arrest data (subsample)	Study B arrest data (total sample; Ashton et al., 2021)
Assault	51%	91%	69%
Criminal damage	77%	82%	54%
Fighting alone	89%	–	–
Fighting group	72%	–	–
Affray	–	22%	25%
Public order sect. 4 (threats)	–	60%	45%
Domestic violence	–	14%	10%

shows an increase in the percentages of those who were arrested for assault, criminal damage, and public order section 4 offenses. Details of these offenses indicate a reactive response, mostly toward peers or rivals, but in the case of three of the young people the focus of the assault and criminal damage of property belonging to family members (parents and siblings).

Risk Factors Associated with Expressive Violent Offenses (EVO)

A US study revealed that 77% of violent victimizations were committed by adolescents acting alone and 71% occurred with their peers (Oudekerk & Morgan, 2016). However, the same authors found that assault was specifically associated with solo offenders. When the total sample for Study B is considered Table 3.1) most EVOs (except for arson) were committed by individuals. As noted in Chapter 1, the motivations for arson are multiple (Canter & Fritzon, 1998). The autonomy associated with other offenses can be partly explained by a lack of impulse control, as described by the case study in Box 3.1.

Impulse control is a developmental risk factor with a strong relationship to violent behaviors (Masten & Cicchetti, 2010; Piquero et al., 2007). Steinberg and Cauffman's (1996) model of psychosocial development recognized three discreet factors: temperance (impulse control and suppression of aggression); perspective (consideration of others and future orientation); and responsibility (personal responsibility and resistance to peers). The relationship of these risk factors to adolescent offending is well documented in the research (Monahan et al., 2013). Researchers who studied a sample of court referred youth as part of a community program suggested that lower levels of anger, impulse control, and empathy may be associated with recidivism (Balkin et al., 2011). A study exploring the levels of self-control in a sample containing both persistent and non-career criminals found that low self-control was a significant predictor for continued offending (DeLisi & Vaughan, 2008). Impulse control is a dynamic risk factor, and targeted interventions have been shown to significantly increase the ability of children and adolescents to control their impulsivity (Piquero et al., 2010). This is an important finding, since higher impulse control interacts with other key risk and protective factors (Pratt, 2016).

However, the relationship between impulsivity and environmental risk factors associated with EVOs, such as home, school, and neighborhood, is not straightforward (Fine et al., 2016). Researchers using longitudinal data supported prior studies to show that low impulse control is associated with higher levels of delinquency among adolescents (Fine et al., 2016). Whereas previous studies (Chen & Jacobson, 2013) indicated that a positive or pro-social environment could increase impulse control, the later study did not support this relationship. The authors' explanation cited other research on the influence of a young person's behavior on the actors they encounter in their environment. That young people who are viewed as aggressive might be treated differently. The authors consider that there may be other confounding factors that influence whether a young person becomes less impulsive. Central to this would be the impact of additional exposure to violence for those young people who witness or experience this through their involvement in gangs and/or groups (Ashton et al., 2020).

Certainly, the home can play an important role as either a risk or a protective factor for aggressive responses and violence. When the total cohort for Study B is considered, 55% of the young people came from homes with at least one early domestic violence callout, and this percentage increased to 100% for the most prolific offenders from that sample, thus increasing the number of adverse childhood experiences (ACEs) and trauma. A review of the literature on the impact of DV on children found that victims were at increased risk of developing emotional and behavioral problems (Holt et al., 2008). The authors cite research to indicate that mothers who are victims of DV often struggle to control their children as they grow older, and who in turn aggress their mother and family (McCloskey & Lichter, 2003).

Assault

There are three legal categories of assault in England and Wales (Sentencing Council, 2022). Common assault – when a person inflicts violence on someone or makes them think that they will be attacked, includes verbal and spitting at someone. Actual bodily harm (ABH) – causes hurt or injury to the victim, including psychological harm. The hurt does not need to be serious or permanent but must be more than "trifling". Grievous bodily harm (GBH) – intent to cause injury or that injury was likely to occur. Wounding – less serious than GBH, the victim's skin is broken.

Assault was a common arrest for young people in Studies A and B and clustered with criminal damage in terms of arrests and self-reported behaviors Figures 1.1 and 1.2). When the total sample for study B was considered, assault was also associated with public order section 4 offenses and possession of cannabis (Ashton et al., 2021). Further analysis of these data indicated that assault was significantly correlated with section 4 public order offenses and criminal damage, suggesting a lack of impulse control in this group of offenders.

Although most young people who were arrested for common assault aged out of this behavior by the time they were in late adolescence, this was not the case for the Study B subsample. This cohort showed a progression from common assault to grievous bodily harm, as illustrated by Box 3.2. It is clear from this case study that there were several extenuating factors in addition to reactive aggressive responses. These were exposure to domestic violence, his mother's addiction problems and inability to support him, removal from the family home at a young age, multiple drug use during early adolescence, and external victimization with exposure to violence by association with organized crime groups. The outcomes for this young person were not determined from the start, but it is easy to see that they were consequential. This example demonstrates the importance of supporting families who are exposed to domestic violence beyond the removal of the perpetrator. It also acts as a reminder that the young person was a victim himself. As with other cases from those who offended the most in Study B subsample, criminal involvement and victimization were generational, illustrating the need for family focused support in addition to working with the young person.

BOX 3.2 STUDY B SUBSAMPLE: A TYPICAL CASE STUDY ILLUSTRATING EXPRESSIVE VIOLENCE AS A STARTING POINT

Young people placed in care before adolescence due to domestic violence at home and parental substance addiction. Begin using cannabis and cocaine during early adolescence. Early reactive responses toward the caregiver (usually mother) included destroying her property and hitting her. The assaults also extend to vulnerable strangers who are unable to defend themselves and from the arrest reports these were without any provocation or reason. The level of violence escalates during mid-adolescence with an assault using a weapon. This can also include violence against staff in a residential home. Behavior is typically triggered by being refused something. Violence becomes a learned behavior and is then used for income-generating offenses when with other people. These associations then lead to becoming a victim of modern slavery through involvement with drug trafficking and county lines.

Risk Factors Associated with Assault

With the complex needs of the young person in case summary in Box 3.2 in mind, it is helpful to consider both the professional and self-assessed risk for the total cohort of Study B. Figure 3.1 shows the relationship between professional risk assessment on the AssetPlus forms for the cohort. Not surprisingly anger and violent behavior were in the same region of the plot, along with problems attending school, use of time, and drug use. Also in this region were domestic violence logs. As with the summary illustrated in Figure 3.1, assault, anger, use of time, low school attendance, and drug use are responses. DV at home and the associated trauma are the reality of the young people's lives. Although all are listed as risk factors, they require different support. It would be wrong to assume causality of DV, this situation needs to be addressed both in terms of the impact of past trauma and, where relevant, the continuation of this environmental and psychological risk in the form of further exposure to violence.

The importance of taking DV into consideration when supporting a young person who acts aggressively toward others is further supported by an additional analysis. A chi-squared test of independence was also performed to examine the relationship between arrest for assault and professional risk assessment. Significant relationships were found with history of domestic violence callouts on the police database X (1, $N = 171$) = 8.84, $p = .003$; young person controlling/influencing peers X^2 (1, $N = 159$) = 6.17, $p = .01$; and a diagnosis of ADHD X^2(1, $N = 158$) = 4.95, $p = .03$.

The influencing of peers supports the example cited in the first case study (Box 3.1) and shows how an individual with low levels of impulse control can impact upon a group's involvement with violent offending. This supports prior research on the escalation of violence within a group offense (Conway & McCord, 2002). Attention deficit hyperactivity disorder (ADHD) is a common neurodevelopmental disorder among children and young people. In the samples under consideration in the present book, it manifests as an inability to control impulsive behaviors or overactivity. The condition is treatable with medication, but studies have shown that the family are central to supporting a young person with their treatment and that patients stop because of unpleasant side effects (Charach & Fernandez, 2013).

To investigate whether any of these factors could predict an arrest for assault a logistic regression analysis was performed. None of the professional risk factors that were associated with assault predicted an arrest for the offense. However, when the equivalent self-assessed risk factors did predict assault, the only variable to make a unique contribution was the young person's perception that their family didn't care; this supports the need for including the family in any intervention (see below).

The relationship between assault and self-assessed risk by the young people offers a clear insight into the extent of familial concern (Figure 3.2). Assault was associated with being in trouble with their family, staying away from home, arguments at home, and feeling of anger. It is important to note

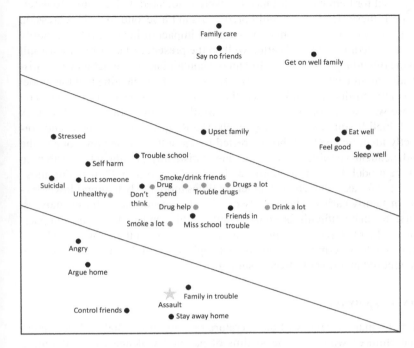

Figure 3.2 Study B total sample: The relationship between self-assessed risk and assault
Coefficient of alienation = 0.19.

that irrespective of other risk factors, for the young people in the total sample from Study B, the home was a problem. Also in this region was controlling friends, supporting the previous findings.

To determine if these risk factors could predict assault a logistic regression analysis was then performed to assess the impact of: feeling angry, controlling friends, members of the family in trouble, staying away from home and arguments at home, on the presence of an arrest for assault. The full model was not significant, and none of the risk factors predicted assault. So further statistical analysis was undertaken to explore the relationship between an arrest for assault and all self-assessed risk factors using Pearson product-moment correlation coefficient. There was a weak, negative correlation between assault and: Family caring $r = -.17$, $n = 172$, $p = .05$; needing help with drug use $r = -.18$, $n = 172$, $p = .04$; and eating well $r = -.21$, $n = 172$, $p < .02$. Risk factors were all lower for those with assault arrests, so significantly lower levels of eating well, family caring, and identifying the need for help with substance use were associated with assault. To determine if these risk factors could predict assault a second logistic regression analysis was then performed to assess the impact of lower levels of: family caring, needing help, and eating well on the presence of an arrest for assault in the offending profiles. The full model containing all predictors was statistically significant, X^2 (3, N = 172) = 15.76, $p < .01$, indicating that the model was able to distinguish between those who were arrested for assault and those who were not. The model as a whole explained between 11% (Cox and Snell R square) and 16% (Nagelkerke R squared) of variance and correctly identified 68% of those arrested for assault. As noted only one of the independent variables made a unique statistically significant contribution to the model, less caring family with an odds ratio of 5.92, meaning those arrested for assault were just under six times more likely to report lower levels of family caring. There are two points to consider from these analyses. First, it can be difficult for young people to fully understand what is impacting on their behavior. Second, all the analyses suggest that violence at home can have long-term impact on young people and their behavior. This cannot be ignored in terms of offering support.

DV Perpetrators

A meta-analytic review of the literature relating to familial violence found that children who were the victims of parental violence were 71% more likely to become perpetrators of violence toward their parents themselves (Gallego et al., 2019). Victimization by a parent was found to be correlated to child to parent violence more highly than exposure to other forms of violence (Contreras & del Carmen Cano, 2016). Among the arrestees from Study B subsample 14% of the young people were arrested for DV (Table 3.1). However, since 100% of young people in this sample were victims of DV at some point in their lives, the figures could be much higher. This is because research has indicated that child to parent violence remains underreported, due to fear, guilt, and defensiveness (Arce et al., 2015; Gallego et al., 2019). The arrests in Study B occurred as the young people reached mid-to-late adolescence, possibly because behavior that had hitherto been dealt with by the family had become more of a threat due to an escalation of aggression or because as the young person grew physically stronger, they became more of a perceived threat. In most cases the arrest record describes the young person being refused something or a parent being critical of their behavior. In this sense the violent response is reactive rather than coercive or controlling and mimics aggressive behavior toward external stimuli.

Criminal Damage

Criminal damage in England is defined as unlawfully damaging or destroying the property of another person and includes recklessness leading to this outcome. As a criminal act it can be used expressively or instrumentally. Early arrest records and early adolescent self-reported narratives show that criminal damage charges are often the result of a thrill-seeking activity gone wrong. Examples Study C include playing with fireworks (Box 5.1) and breaking into an abandoned building site (Box 6.4). Arrest records from Study B total sample, however, indicated that fireworks and break-ins can also be linked to instrumental criminal damage. On one occasion a child threw fireworks into a house because the occupants had complained about him. On another occasion a young person set fire to his school because he had been excluded; the fire setting was days after the event that provoked the behavior. In other instances, young people committed acts of vandalism, typically in groups, and often in response to boredom.

Criminal damage, like arson (which can be the method), therefore covers a range of motivations and categories of violence toward property (Figure 3.3). There is a behavioral difference between responding to damaging property as an act of revenge and because of a thrill-seeking behavior to relieve boredom. As with assault, for those young people who escalate their violence, the use of criminal damage can change as the person ages. Generally, early reactive criminal damage is present on the timelines of those young people who damage property for instrumental purposes. It is possible that just as they see an assault working effectively to punish someone or to obtain what they want, criminal damage is another successful means of threatening someone or revenge. Another distinction can be made between criminal damage as an expressive/reactive solo offense and group criminal damage, which can be coincidental as an early behavior. The arrest data suggest that those who commit criminal damage reactively are more likely to continue to use it instrumentally. As they aged, the young people who desisted from this behavior typically had an arrest for criminal damage because of another incident, for example, breaking into an abandoned building.

Some conditions can lead to all four categories of criminal damage. A young person's solo arrest record from Study B demonstrates this co-occurrence. During early adolescence he was arrested for expressive violence in the form of public order offenses, knife carrying, assaults on authority figures, and criminal damage relating to a prank. As he aged into mid-adolescence, he was charged with DV, including criminal damage and assault against family members and a former girlfriend. After leaving home he continued to aggress family members when they disappointed him in some way.

Figure 3.3 Categories of criminal damage

Fighting

Fighting can be expressive or instrumental and can also fulfill both motivations. The self-reported data from Study A demonstrated a high percentage of both solo (89%) and group fighting (72%) among the sample. Both forms of fighting were in the early expressive region of the offending plot, along with criminal damage, assault, weapon carrying, and graffiti (Figure 1.2). The narrative of a young person from Study C (see Chapter 1 depressed victim narrative) described friends coercing the young person into attending a fight with a rival group; soon after arriving he was alarmed to see that the opponents had weapons and fled the scene (Ashton & Bussu, 2020). The motivation was an ongoing feud between young people from different areas, and in this respect the group's response was expressive.

In both the narratives and the arrest data, fighting alone was like assault in that it was typically a reaction to a stimulus such as name-calling or encountering someone from a prior dispute, often from a group fight. Initiating a fight can also serve an instrumental purpose in that it can give a young person who is involved with groups who offend social credibility and status (Warr, 2002). In the police data fighting was a means to an arrest for a related offense, such as assault. The fact that fighting in the self-reported data was as high as assault and criminal damage suggests that the motivations and co-occurrence of these offenses are linked behaviorally.

Sexual Offenses

Sexual offenses (Table 3.2) rarely appear in the arrest data for Studies A and B. When they do, they are associated with more serious offenses (Figures 1.1 and 1.2) and appear later in offending trajectories (Ashton et al., 2021).

Table 3.2 Study B total sample: Offending style for expressive violent arrests

Offense	Solo	Peer co	Older co
Assault	253	38	30
DV perp.	27	0	1
Affray	18	6	5
Public order sect. 4	31	10	3
Criminal damage	150	38	13
Sexual offenses	17	5	2
Arson	4	6	4
Malicious com.	5	0	0

The only exception to this observation is when a young person had a single arrest for a sexual offense, and they were not otherwise involved in criminal behavior. Sexual offending therefore appears at opposite ends of the offending spectrum. This can likely be explained by different motivations and thus demonstrates that assessing a single offense category in isolation can be misleading. It is also unlikely to inform the most appropriate support or intervention. Offenses in the Study B subsample data show opportunistic incidents, often focused on victims who have additional vulnerabilities (intoxicated or substantially younger).

Summary and Implications for Practice

EVO is typically a reactive response to a situation. This behavior can be due to a lack of impulse control or learned. Both explanations can be associated with childhood trauma and adverse childhood experiences. Assault is typically committed alone or can be instigated by a single member of a group in response to a stimulus. Young people who committed significantly more offenses than their peers (Study B subsample) escalated the seriousness of their assaults as they aged. A small percentage of this sample also became domestic violence perpetrators, although parents are unlikely to report this phenomenon, so the figures are likely to be higher. Criminal damage can be reactive or instrumental; an important point when considering the most appropriate intervention for young people who destroy or damage property.

It is also worth noting that the young people from Study C who described an earlier case of reactive assault were able to reflect on their behavior and said that they would no longer respond in this way. For some early adolescents, reactive aggression is their default, in some cases only a way to express their feelings of frustration. Furthermore, the young people who committed expressive offenses typically said that they were conscious of their adrenaline levels rising and the sensation of anger. Psychological support to help young people control their feelings of anger and to express their frustrations verbally could prevent the escalation of aggressive behaviors.

68 *Expressive Violence*

References

Arce, R., Fariña, F., Seijo, D., & Novo, M. (2015). Assessing impression management with the MMPI-2 in child custody litigation. *Assessment, 22*(6), 769–777.

Ashton, S. A., & Bussu, A. (2020). Peer groups, street gangs and organised crime in the narratives of adolescent male offenders. *Journal of Criminal Psychology, 10*(4).

Ashton, S.-A., Ioannou, M., & Hammond, L. (forthcoming). Applying the criminal narrative roles and emotions to young people who offend in groups.

Ashton, S. A., Ioannou, M., Hammond, L., & Synnott, J. (2020). The relationship of offending style to psychological and social risk factors in a sample of adolescent males. *Journal of Investigative Psychology and Offender Profiling, 17*(2), 76–92.

Ashton, S. A., Valentine, M., & Chan, B. (2021). Differentiating categories of violent adolescent offending and the associated risks in police and youth offending service records. *International Journal of Offender Therapy and Comparative Criminology*, 0306624X211058960.

Balkin, R. S., Miller, J., Ricard, R. J., Garcia, R., & Lancaster, C. (2011). Assessing factors in adolescent adjustment as precursors to recidivism in court-referred youth. *Measurement and Evaluation in Counseling and Development, 44*(1), 52–59.

Canter, D., & Fritzon, K. (1998). Differentiating arsonists: A model of firesetting actions and characteristics. *Legal and Criminological Psychology, 3*(1), 73–96.

Charach, A., & Fernandez, R. (2013). Enhancing ADHD medication adherence: Challenges and opportunities. *Current Psychiatry Reports, 15*(7), 1–8.

Chen, P., & Jacobson, K. C. (2013). Impulsivity moderates promotive environmental influences on adolescent delinquency: A comparison across family, school, and neighborhood contexts. *Journal of Abnormal Child Psychology, 41*(7), 1133–1143.

Condry, R., & Miles, C. (2013). *Adolescent to parent violence: Key findings for police services.* Economic and Social Research Council.

Contreras, L., & del Carmen Cano, M. (2016). Child-to-parent violence: The role of exposure to violence and its relationship to social-cognitive processing. *European Journal of Psychology Applied to Legal Context, 8*(2), 43–50.

Conway, K. P., & McCord, J. (2002). A longitudinal examination of the relation between co-offending with violent accomplices and violent crime. *Aggressive Behavior, 28*(2), 97–108.

DeLisi, M., Piquero, A. R., & Cardwell, S. M. (2016). The unpredictability of murder: Juvenile homicide in the pathways to desistance study. *Youth Violence and Juvenile Justice, 14*(1), 26–42.

DeLisi, M., & Vaughn, M. G. (2008). The Gottfredson-Hirschi critiques revisited: Reconciling self-control theory, criminal careers, and career criminals. *International Journal of Offender Therapy and Comparative Criminology, 52*(5), 520–537.

Fine, A., Mahler, A., Steinberg, L., Frick, P. J., & Cauffman, E. (2017). Individual in context: The role of impulse control on the association between the home, school, and neighborhood developmental contexts and adolescent delinquency. *Journal of Youth and Adolescence*, *46*(7), 1488–1502.

Gallego, R., Novo, M., Fariña, F., & Arce, R. (2019). Child-to-parent violence and parent-to-child violence: A meta-analytic review. *European Journal of Psychology Applied to Legal Context*, *11*(2), 51–59.

Holt, S., Buckley, H., & Whelan, S. (2008). The impact of exposure to domestic violence on children and young people: A review of the literature. *Child Abuse and Neglect*, *32*(8), 797–810.

Kiesler, C. A., & Kiesler, S. B. (1970). *Conformity*. Addison-Wesley.

Masten, A. S., & Cicchetti, D. (2010). Developmental cascades. *Development and Psychopathology*, *22*(3), 491–495.

McCloskey, L. A., & Lichter, E. L. (2003). The contribution of marital violence to adolescent aggression across different relationships. *Journal of Interpersonal Violence*, *18*(4), 390–412.

Monahan, K. C., Steinberg, L., Cauffman, E., & Mulvey, E. P. (2013). Psychosocial (im)maturity from adolescence to early adulthood: Distinguishing between adolescence-limited and persisting antisocial behavior. *Development and Psychopathology*, *25*(4pt1), 1093–1105.

Oudekerk, B., & Morgan, R. E. (2016). *Co-offending among adolescents in violent victimizations, 2004–13*. US Department of Justice, Office of Justice Programs, Bureau of Justice Statistics.

Piquero, A. R., Daigle, L. E., Gibson, C., Piquero, N. L., & Tibbetts, S. G. (2007). Research note: are life-course-persistent offenders at risk for adverse health outcomes? *Journal of Research in Crime and Delinquency*, *44*(2), 185–207.

Piquero, A. R., Jennings, W. G., & Farrington, D. P. (2010). On the malleability of self-control: Theoretical and policy implications regarding a general theory of crime. *Justice Quarterly*, *27*(6), 803–834.

Pratt, T. C. (2016). A self-control/life-course theory of criminal behavior. *European Journal of Criminology*, *13*(1), 129–146.

Sentencing Council. (2022). Retrieved October 1, 2022 from https://www.sentencingcouncil.org.uk.

Steinberg, L., & Cauffman, E. (1996). Maturity of judgment in adolescence: Psychosocial factors in adolescent decision making. *Law and Human Behavior*, *20*(3), 249–272.

Warr, M. (2002). *Companions in crime: The social aspects of criminal conduct*. Cambridge University Press.

4   Knife Crime

Box 4.1 is an interview with a young person from Study C. He was 14 at the time of the incident that he described and was accompanied by two younger family members. The offense he described was robbery of a mobile phone. He explained the background and the incident relating to the knife. The case study illustrates two important points relating to the carrying of knives. First, the young person was carrying it with the intention of getting revenge and cited prior violent experiences with the targeted group. Second, he was with two other individuals, but they were younger than him and all three were considerably younger than the targets. Third, although he carried a knife (in fact a machete that he had acquired), he only needed to reference it, rather than use it or show it, to get the opportunistic victim to relinquish his phone. Finally, he described throwing the phone away as soon as he had taken it; the offense was more an act of punishment and/or a show of power rather than income generating.

BOX 4.1 STUDY C: CASE STUDY OF KNIFE CARRYING

"Just a fight happened. Two fights happened actually but with the first fight, it started over me actually … and this kid was getting bad to me and this was years and years … this was like three, four years ago. And he started getting bad to me, telling me like just loads of shit and then I arranged a fight with [person].

We've gone up and there was a big group of them, and there was only like four, five of us, six of us and we all ran off and we've chased them and we ended up catching one of them but he had a big bar and he hit one of my mates in the stomach with the bar and he ended up getting leathered and they still was getting bad after that and we ended up going meeting them again, well no we was supposed to

---

DOI: 10.4324/9781003255697-5

go and meet them, we met them the day after and no one shown up 'cause this was ... it was older people who came this time. And then a year later or something, it started getting bad and we ended meeting them and then [pause] we went and met them and we was with loads ... I remember just the street was full of just older people and I didn't hardly even knew them and like they were telling me names and then probably know me names now, do you know what I mean? They were like nineteen year olds and I was only fourteen so.

Well yeah. I asked him [robbery victim] did you know a couple of people and he said, 'Yeah.' I said, 'Where are they?' [he said] 'I don't know' and I just leathered him, innit. He wasn't going to, he wasn't telling, he was trying that. I don't know and then I had a blade hid in my pants but I didn't pull it out, I just told him 'cause there's no point, I probably already scared him enough, do you know what I mean?"

(17 years old. Other offenses included robbery with a weapon, used a card illegally, stole a car, sold cannabis and class A drugs; handled stolen goods, carried a weapon, fighting, assault, criminal damage, arson, daily use of cannabis.)

Knife Carrying and Knife Crime

The term "knife crime" includes knife carrying and the use of a knife as part of an offense (Foster, 2013). The broader legal term of "bladed article" encompasses other items that have a blade or are sharply pointed (except for a folding pocketknife). Research on a sample of 318 people under the age of 21 in the UK who were charged with murder found that knives were the most common weapon, followed by bottles (Gerard et al., 2017). Of that sample, only three young people used a firearm to commit homicide. Earlier research on knife carrying in London identified other everyday objects ranging from snooker balls to sharpened plastic pens (Lemos, 2004) as weapons.

Firearm access is more restricted in the UK than some other countries. For the participants in Study C firearm access was restricted and is usually indicative of an association with organized crime members, even if those people are at street level. However, researchers have warned against associating all firearms with gang involvement and have pointed out the distinction between the use of weapons "professionally" and as a part of street-level criminality for both purpose and status (Hallsworth & Silverstone,

2009). This latter group, the authors observed, would utilize any form of weapon to support their activities. It could be argued that an adolescent would need to have the necessary criminal associations (peer or adult) to obtain a firearm. In all three studies for the current publication knife carrying as a behavior is different from use of firearms and indicates earlier stages of violent offending.

Equally knife crime does not fall into a single behavioral category, which is why an analysis of knife use for Study B total sample did not find a specific association with other behaviors (Ashton et al., 2021). Studies and official records rarely describe a knife in enough detail to distinguish between the source and type. Behaviorally there is a difference between taking an available knife from the family home compared to purchasing a hunting-knife online or being given such a knife by a criminal contact. The outcome and risk are of course the same (serious wounding or death), but how the young person acquired the knife can be insightful in understanding their motivation and purpose. Like other offenses, weapon carrying can be either expressive or instrumental (Sheley & Wright, 1993 on gun carrying). It has been suggested that young males carry knives for different reasons, including a perceived need for protection, fear of crime, and to enhance their status (Riggs & Palasinksi, 2011). More generally, knife carrying has been associated with peer antisocial influence and instrumental offending and protection (Dijkstra et al., 2012).

A systematic review of offender characteristics relating to knife crime (Browne et al., 2022) found the following factors were associated with juvenile knife carrying: exposure to violence (as a witness, victim, or perpetrator) and illegal substance use (excluding cannabis). A second review focused on young people (Haylock et al., 2020) found that adverse childhood experiences, school exclusion, mental illness (depression, suicide, and self-harm), and prior victimization were associated with knife crime. Research in France found that prior victimization, negative maternal relationship, and repeating a grade at school increased the odds of weapon carrying (Bégue et al., 2016). However, the sample for the study was a general population rather than focused on young people who are involved in offending behaviors.

In the case of juveniles, there are a range of social pressures that researchers have identified for knife carrying. These include the role of peer or group pressure (Lemos, 2004), a perceived lack of confidence in the policing in inner-city areas (Riggs & Palasinski, 2011). In the case of young males, researchers have suggested that masculinity plays a role in the decision to carry a knife (Deuchar, 2016) forming part of a lifestyle (Harding, 2020) and the associated social fate to generate "street capital" (Harding, 2012).

In the UK knife carrying is often associated with gang membership and the related activities of drug selling, fighting rivals, protecting areas, and threatening people with violence (Harding, 2020). Lemos (2004) identified that there is evidence to support group influence but not a gang effect at the time of writing. A study in Edinburgh also showed that the risk factors associated with knife crime and gang membership were different. Knife carrying was associated with self-harm, social isolation, low self-esteem, and lack of parental support (McVie, 2010). In contrast, young people who were gang-involved were associated with social disadvantage and high-crime areas. This study also found young people who self-reported knife carrying were more likely to have committed criminal damage, theft, and violent offenses compared to young people who did not carry a weapon in the sample. Analysis of the full cohort associated with Study B (Ashton et al., 2021) indicated that in self-assessment of risk knife crime was associated with missing school, family upset, friends who get into trouble and were in the same region of an SSA plot as assault. Social changes mean that the influences on knife carrying can be fluid. However, data from the three studies for the current publication do not support a strong relationship between gang membership per se and knife crime. These data suggest that there are individual characteristics with a stronger relationship.

Knife Crime in the UK

Knife crime in the UK represents a unique problem that is interwoven with local social problems, access to weapons, and justice responses to the carrying of weapons. For these reasons, some scholars have been critical of drawing on international comparisons to understand what has been deemed a public health problem in the UK (Browne et al., 2022; Haylock, 2020). Given the perceived scale of the problem and the focus of government's strategies toward serious violence (HM Government, 2018), relatively little research has been undertaken on the subject.

If we consider the past decade of knife/offensive weapon crimes resulting in a caution or sentence, young people under the age of 18 years committed between 16% and 21% of this category of offense (YJB, 2021). In the year ending April 2021, 97% of 3,500 cases were for carrying, rather than using, a weapon. The number of hospital admissions for stab wounds from the same period was 180 incidents for under 16-year-olds, and 514 incidents for 16- to 18-year-olds. The percentage of total admissions was lower than the arrest records at 15%. This can perhaps be explained by the low numbers of young people arrested for using a knife, as opposed to carrying.

In the self-reported data from Study A, 61% of the young people said that they had carried a knife (Figure 1.2). However, there was considerable variance regarding the number of times they reported carrying a knife/ weapon; the average number of times that the group carried was 26.14, with a range of 0 to 832 and a standard deviation of 94. Figure 1.2 also demonstrates that weapon carrying was associated with expressive violence (assault, destroying property, fighting, graffiti). It was also close to the income-generating offenses (handling stolen goods, shoplifting, sold cannabis).

As noted, knife carrying is often associated with gang involvement in the UK (Harding, 2020; Haylock et al., 2020), even though internationally weapon carrying is more closely linked to solo offending. Research in the United States identified that adolescent and young adult offenders were more likely to use a weapon when engaging in serious violent acts alone (Oudekerk & Morgan, 2016). Furthermore, gang research in the United States (Ashton et al., 2018) found that some gang leavers commit more offenses than those who remain in the gang, presumably because they have more autonomy and have expand their offending networks beyond a single group.

A binomial logistic regression using data from Study A supported the US findings. This was performed to ascertain the effects of moral disengagement, impulsive irresponsible traits, self-reported offending frequency, and street gang activities on knife carrying. These variables are associated with both knife crime and gang membership as autonomous behaviors and were also found to decrease as risk factors following an intervention for young people from this sample (Ashton & Ward, 2022). The model explained 71% (Nagelkerke R^2) of the variance in knife carrying and correctly classified 82.3% of the young people who self-reported carrying a knife. Higher levels of moral disengagement ($p = .004$), impulsive irresponsible traits ($p = .03$), and higher self-reported offending ($p = .03$) added significantly to the model, but street gang activities did not make a significant contribution.

Official data may tell a different story, simply because as young people progress their offending behaviors, and when they become involved with older criminals, they learn to conceal any weapons close by rather than carrying them. This was described by a participant in Study C regarding the dealing of class A drugs, and it accords with prior research that found both peers and "Olders/Elders" train young people how to use a knife to cause the most harm (Harding, 2020). Study C also supports an earlier study that found most young people stop carrying a knife by the age of 17, but those who persisted tended to carry more frequently (McVie, 2010). The link to older offenders and training may explain why weapon carrying in the arrest data from Study B subsample (Figure 1.1) was associated with income-generating crimes (theft, burglary, theft of a motor vehicle, possession with intent to supply class B drugs). Figure 1.5 indicated that carrying a weapon was associated with offenders who were around five years older than the young people (early- to mid-20s). In this sample of late adolescents and young adults, a lower percentage (55%) of this sample had been arrested for weapon carrying.

Using data from the total cohort associated with Study B subsample (Ashton et al., 2021), a chi-squared test of independence was performed to examine the association between knife crime and other offenses. Significant relationships were found with burglary (χ^2 (1, N = 172) = 15.17, p = .000), theft of a motor vehicle (χ^2 (1, N = 172) = 8.53, p = .003), motoring offenses (χ^2 (1, N = 172) = 8.97, p = .003), a section 4 public order offense, which is fear or provocation of violence (χ^2 (1, N = 172) = 4.54, p = .003), and possession of cannabis (χ^2 (1, N = 172) = 4.48, p = .03). The strongest relationship was between a knife offense and burglary. This does not necessarily mean that people use a knife while committing a burglary, nor is it causal. It is helpful to see that these behaviors co-occur on the timelines of young people who have been arrested for knife offenses. In fact, these findings support previous research that found an association between knife crime and increased violence and assault (McVie, 2010).

Stages of Knife Crime

If we refer to the case study at the start of this chapter, it is possible to see that there are stages relating to knife crime (Figure 4.1). Box 4.1 shows a suggested pathway of knife crime based on the three studies. The young person reported initially carrying a knife for protection from a rival group (stage 1). Some young people report being told to carry a knife for others within their group. There are elements of the three stages in the buildup to incident that he described. The weapon had also become part of his identity as someone who could intimidate people (stage 2) and he carried a knife routinely (stage 3) but had moved to stage 4, using knife with control and instrumentally when necessary. There is also a factor relating to the successful outcome of knife carrying that reinforces the need or desire to continue. For those who experience negative consequences (arrest, trauma) from carrying or using a knife, or who receive an intervention, this can lead to desistance. However, the further the stage, the harder it is likely to be for a young person to understand the dangers or negative consequences of their behaviors. This is because knife carrying, or use, becomes more normalized (Harding, 2020).

For the young person in this case study even the knowledge that he had a knife gave him confidence in dealing with his victim and caused enough fear that he did not need to present it as a threat. His comment that he had "probably scared him enough by then" illustrates this and shows a degree

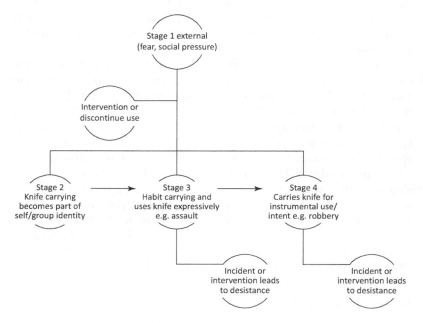

Figure 4.1 Model for knife carrying and use

of restraint and control. As with the stages from expressive to instrumental violent offending, each of the knife carrying and use phases requires different levels of intervention. For the two younger observers this incident reinforced the social capital of weapon carrying. As young people become more entrenched with criminal associates, irrespective of the stage that they are at, they learn the value of using a knife instrumentally. This training reinforces the potential and power of carrying and using a knife.

Summary and Implications for Practice

Although many studies frame knife crime within gang membership, research has not necessarily found a strong associated between the two behaviors. We can, however, view knife crime in key stages and suggest different ways to explore risk when working with young people. In this regard key questions that would be helpful to ask, where did the young person get the knife/weapon? Was it was purchased online illegally (by them or given to them), or obtained opportunistically? What was the reason they first started carrying (fear or social pressure)? For some young people seeing the risk that knife carrying poses will be difficult to comprehend. This is especially true of those who have reached stage 4 and who use weapons instrumentally, as an effective means of protecting themselves and/or obtaining status, income, or revenge. It is also worth considering whether the young person is being forced or coerced into carrying a knife for another person.

Understanding the reasons for and the rewards of knife carrying is central to any intervention. Generic campaigns warning of the dangers of knife carrying are not likely to impact young people who are in stages 3 and 4. Rather, references to potential violence are likely to have the opposite effect and encourage some young people to carry a bladed article. Targeted interventions that consider a young person's rationale for knife carrying are essential for maximum impact. It should also be noted that the stages that are identified in Figure 4.1 can escalate rapidly, even during supervision for a different offense.

References

Ashton, S.-A., Ioannou, M., & Hammond, L. (2018). Offending patterns of youth gang members and leavers. *Journal of Gang Research, 25*(2), 29–49.

Ashton, S. A., Valentine, M., & Chan, B. (2021). Differentiating categories of violent adolescent offending and the associated risks in police and youth offending service records. *International Journal of Offender Therapy and Comparative Criminology*, 0306624X211058960

Ashton, S.-A., & Ward, J. (2022). Bridging the gap between criminal psychology and frontline youthwork: A case study in programme development and evaluation. *Assessment and Development Matters, 14*(4), 15–20.

Bègue, L., Roché, S., & Duke, A. A. (2016). Young and armed: A cross-sectional study on weapon carrying among adolescents. *Psychology, Crime and Law, 22*(5), 455–472.

Browne, K. D., Green, K., Jareno-Ripoll, S., & Paddock, E. (2022). Knife crime offender characteristics and interventions–A systematic review. *Aggression and Violent Behavior*, 101774, 2–14.

Deuchar, R. (2016). Scottish youth gangs. In H. Croall, G. Mooney, & M. Munro (Eds.), *Crime, justice and society in Scotland* (pp. 67–81). Routledge.

Dijkstra, J. K., Gest, S. D., Lindenberg, S., Veenstra, R., & Cillessen, A. H. (2012). Testing three explanations of the emergence of weapon carrying in peer context: The roles of aggression, victimization, and the social network. *Journal of Adolescent Health, 50*(4), 371–376.

Foster, R. (2013). *Knife crime interventions: What works'?* The Scottish Centre for Crime and Justice Research Research Report 02. SCCJR.

Gerard, F. J., Browne, K. D., & Whitfield, K. C. (2017). Gender comparison of young people charged with murder in England and Wales. *International Journal of Offender Therapy and Comparative Criminology, 61*(4), 413–429.

Hallsworth, S., & Silverstone, D. (2009). 'That's life innit' a British perspective on guns, crime and social order. *Criminology and Criminal Justice*, *9*(3), 359–377.

Harding, S. (2012). A reputational extravaganza? The role of the urban street gang in the riots in London: Simon Harding argues that the social networks of urban street gangs played a central role. *Criminal Justice Matters*, *87*(1), 22–23.

Harding, S. (2020). *County lines: Exploitation and drug dealing among urban street gangs*. Policy Press.

Haylock, S., Boshari, T., Alexander, E. C., Kumar, A., Manikam, L., & Pinder, R. (2020). Risk factors associated with knife-crime in United Kingdom among young people aged 10–24 years: A systematic review. *BMC Public Health*, *20*(1), 1–19.

HM Government. (2018). *Serious violence strategy*. HM Government.

Lemos, G. (2004). *Fear and fashion: The use of knives and other weapons by young people*. Bridge House Trust, Lemon & Crane.

McVie, S. (2010). *Gang membership and knife carrying: Findings from the Edinburgh study of youth transitions and crime*. The Scottish Government.

Oudekerk, B., & Morgan, R. E. (2016). *Co-offending among adolescents in violent victimizations, 2004–13*. US Department of Justice, Office of Justice Programs, Bureau of Justice Statistics.

Riggs, D. W., & Palasinski, M. (2011). Young men view things differently. *BMJ*, *342*.

Sheley, J. F., & Wright, J. D. (1993). *Gun acquisition and possession in selected juvenile samples*. US Department of Justice, Office of Justice Programs, National Institute of Justice.

YJB. (2021). *Youth justice statistics for 2020 to 2021 for England and Wales*. Youth Justice Board for England and Wales.

5   Sensation Seeking

Introduction

Boredom was commonly cited as a reason for offending by young people in Study C. As a motivation it represents under-arousal; however, it may still act as the catalyst for the initiation of thrill-seeking behaviors (Putniņš, 2010).

BOX 5.1 STUDY C: CASE STUDY RELATING TO FIREWORKS

We were just – we were bored and my mate had fireworks, like, hundred and seventy, like, little rocket things which we just light and throw, so we just went out throwing them. Then my mate threw one onto the road, and then there was a police car there. And it nearly hit the police car. Then they chased us. Then, like, three vans came. They got us. We were just listening to music and then one of my mates says that we were bored, so, like, 'Come and set off some fireworks' and we just went out and did it. Just to have fun. … They just – they put us all in cuffs, searched us all. Luckily we threw the fireworks, 'cause we had a bag of them, so we threw them so they never found them. Took our names, then they took us back to my mate's house in the van, 'cause we all pretended that we live there, and that was it. (14 years old. Other offenses included shoplifting, sold cannabis, robbery with a weapon, fighting, carried a weapon, arson, daily cannabis use.)

DOI: 10.4324/9781003255697-6

Rewards of Crime

Thrill seeking or "sensory incentives motivate human behavior through the desire for novel, pleasurable, stimulating experiences and the avoidance of aversive experiences, including boredom" (Youngs, 2006, p. 3). Zuckerman (1994, p. 27) defined sensation seeking as "A trait defined by the seeking of varied, novel, complex, and intense sensations and experiences, and the willingness to take physical, social, legal, and financial risks for the sake of such experience". Whereas thrill-seeking suggests an immediate gratification, sensory incentives recognize that some behaviors offer indirect and internal rewards (Katz, 1988; Youngs, 2006). Researchers also point out that not all sensation seeking involves risk, but in the case of substance use high sensation seeking may increase drug use and variety (Zuckerman & Aluja, 2015). Like other personality traits thrill seeking is on a continuum, but those who score high have more motivation to offend than their low-scoring counterparts (Burt & Simons, 2013). However, it should be remembered that young people who exhibit these characteristics may suffer from an underlying and undiagnosed disorder. A study found that adolescents who suffered from ADHD and/or conduct disorder were more likely to exhibit lower levels of constraint than their twin (Cukrowicz et al., 2006).

Acquisitive crimes offer an obvious financial reward that, for some, outweighs the risk of getting caught. A quote from 16-year-old participant in Study C suggests a punishment risk and reward assessment known as rational choice framework (Becker, 1968): "Why go do a street robbery that'll get you four years when you can go and do an armed robbery and get you five years. Same charge, same sentence, innit, like it's just stupid". This young person featured in this chapter describing an incident of arson (Box 5.3). However, this was not his only self-reported offense or narrative. He was involved in serious organized crime and violent income-generating offenses (Box 1.3), and his statement reflects the views of adult offenders. This acts as a reminder to consider all the offending behaviors relating to a young person to support their desistance from crime. Research has indicated that the decision to engage in risk-taking behaviors relates to an individual's pleasure arousal in relation to a particular activity (Burt & Simmons, 2013). Other qualitative studies have found that thrill seekers cite fun and feeling good to explain their offending behaviors (Agnew, 1990). A study to investigate risk-taking behavior in a sample of undergraduate students found that higher levels of thrill seeking were associated with property and substance delinquency (Pfefferbaum & Wood, 1994). Interventions to tackle thrill-seeking behaviors may be assisted by finding an alternative activity.

Even for those who seek financial gain from their offending, thrill-seeking activities often involve more than one offender and therefore offer two potential rewards. The first relates to the individual and their group. Examples of this are the social and status gains associated with involvement with organized crime groups, which create an emotional attachment to group membership (Ashton & Bussu, 2020). Second, individual activities can also help to strengthen peer group bonds and group norms. The case studies cited in this chapter indicate that these ties are often weakened when the group is arrested, or an individual escalates the intended behavior. However, group dynamics can impact control and individual rational choices.

Thrill-seeking with Others

Social rewards require the involvement of others, either as actors or as audience; perhaps for this reason many of the crimes that are discussed in this chapter relate to co-offending with peers. Groups offer an additional risk even for individuals with low thrill-seeking traits and as they conform to the in-group identity (Tajfel & Turner, 1982). Box 1.5 illustrates this point. The young person was told "you need to back your boys" in a fight with a rival group and so reluctantly went along. Young people from Study C were able to reflect on their negative peer group relationships during mid-adolescence. Over half of the sample were no longer in contact with the group who they offended with for their chosen crime narrative. This also explains why most adolescent group offenders desist by the time they reach adulthood (Farrington et al., 2008; Moffitt, 1993). Although group offending is often associated with specific roles for those involved, these roles are fluid (Uhnoo, 2016). Furthermore, the following case studies illustrate how an individual with low impulse control or high thrill-seeking motivations can change the nature of an incident for the entire group (Box 5.4).

An analysis of types of deviant group membership from the Study C data revealed three stages of group offending: peer groups, street gangs, and OCG involvement (Ashton & Bussu, 2020). A key difference between peer groups and street gangs was the level of loyalty; peers were often not trusted. This is contrary to previous studies that have found loyalty among temporary groups of friends to avoid rejection (Warr, 2002). In the UK study those who had progressed to membership of a street gang focused on instrumental and income-generating crimes (Ashton & Bussu, 2020). This did not mean that they ceased to react expressively to situations or even that they fully abandoned their peer associations. Participants were able to distinguish between the two groups and purposes, as in the case of one young person (Ashton & Bussu, 2020 participant 10) and Box 1.3 and 5.3. The crimes described in this chapter reflect the peer group activities and peer influence.

Criminal Damage as a Consequential Offense

BOX 5.2 STUDY C: CASE STUDY OF CRIMINAL DAMAGE

It was my mate's birthday so we just went out to get something to eat and afterwards it was like we'd just play football for a bit and then we thought we'd start messing about because we lost our ball. We just picked up stones and started throwing them at random stuff and we just thought it would be funny to start throwing them at the car and the guy was in the car and he just caught one of them [friends] and kept him back, detained him, and waited for the police to come. The police questioned him and then he told the police who was involved and what school I went to, so we got punished in school the next day. (14 years old. Only other offense fighting.)

Chapter 3 considered how damaging property can fulfill different motivations (Figure 3.3). For young people who continue to show signs of aggressive behavior into late adolescence and early adulthood the motivation changes from expressive to instrumental. An arrest or charge for criminal damage can also be a secondary result of another act; often for a young person this was unintentional. Boxes 5.2, 5.3, and 5.4 are all examples where criminal damage charges could appear on a young person's timeline. However, their motivations are all different. Box 5.2 is typical of early adolescent behaviors, where a group of friends are not thinking about the consequences of their behavior. In this example one of the groups began throwing stones and the others joined in because they thought it was "funny". It is possible that there was also a degree of social pressure for other group members to comply with the activity. Common to the theme of sensory offending with others is not thinking about action consequences.

Central to any program intervention is determining whether the young person understands and cares about the potential outcomes of their behavior. If the desire for the social/status/emotional reward is high enough, then any rational choices will be secondary. Group dynamics also present an additional risk during early and mid-adolescence (Warr, 2002). Even here though it is essential to understand whether a young person is an instigator or follower within a particular group. It should also be remembered that such roles are dynamic within the same group and with others. Working with young people to increase their resistance to peer influence is essential for those who are followers. This approach will have little impact on those who are able to influence their peers. Assault was associated with controlling friends in the self-reported risk for the entire cohort of Study B (Figure 3.2). An example of this occurrence was given in the case study featured in Box 3.1, when a young person described how he became angry and the reacted by attacking a group of men who were name calling. His friends joined in the assault when the rival group retaliated.

The evaluation of an intervention for the young people in Study A indicated that moral disengagement was significantly reduced through a tailored intervention with a focus on challenging negative attitudes and behaviors, including peer influence (Ashton & Ward, 2022). Several of the items on Badura's moral disengagement scale, which was used to evaluate program impact, focus on individual responsibility within a group. A change in attitude offers longer-term resilience because it encourages a young person to consider the potential consequences of group actions. Several young people in Study C indicated this when they reflected on their prior group behavior and described a turning point when they decided to disengage with the group (Ashton & Bussu, 2020). Delinquent groups also use loyalty among members as a form of moral cover for their behavior (Warr, 2002). The young person in Box 3.1 reflected that he would behave differently at the time of the interview because he no longer associated with the friends who he was trying to impress when he committed the assault. This change occurred following a targeted intervention program to explore his impulsive behavior and was probably influenced by his maturation.

Arson

BOX 5.3 STUDY C: CASE STUDY OF ARSON

We was all going to smoke weed up there in the back garden and then we had the petrol can 'cause we were filling up the bikes and one of my mates just said, "Let's fucking burn the house down," innit. So we just poured the petrol around the house and burnt it down. It was set up like, you could see it from the bottom of the field and the house on the top of the field and burnt out and then the police all came on the estate and just started nicking [arresting] us and I got away, innit. There was seven of us who went up there to smoke weed in the back garden, just chill and that and we had the "peti" [petrol] can on us so we burnt the house down, but it was abandoned anyway. That's what they all got nicked [arrested] for, innit.

[I was] buzzing like, just a little kid just having a laugh innit thinking, "It's a big fire, that." Just thinking now of it and then when the police come we're all laughing 'cause we got this adrenalin rush 'cause the police are chasing us and then everyone started getting nicked, when I started seeing kids get dragged into "trani" vans that I thought, "Fuck that," and ran home and ran up the field and got through the subways and went home, straight to [road]. Like buzzing that I didn't get caught, innit, tuned my PS4 on and then all my mates like Snapchatted me, "I just got out of [town] police station," and that, they were all like saying how did you not get caught and that, I said, "'Cause I ran up the field on me own and ran through the subways and got away!" (16 years old. Other offenses included robbery with a weapon, used a card illegally, sold cannabis, sold class A drugs, shoplifted, handled stolen goods, fighting, assault, arson, driven under the influence of drugs, carried a weapon, criminal damage, daily use of cannabis, uses cocaine at weekends.) Same participant as Box 1.3.

As noted in Chapter 1, there are multiple motivations for arson (Table 1.1). The narrative in Box 5.3 falls into Canter and Fritzon's (1998) instrumental object category. The group saw the opportunity of an empty house and set fire to it. Prior to this the group had been using off-road bikes illegally and had paused to smoke cannabis. In the second part of his narrative the young person describes himself as "buzzing", "like a little kid", and "having a laugh", thus demonstrating the emotional thrill of seeing the house burning. However, the act also cemented their group identity and shared behavior. One member of the group made the suggestion to set fire to the property, and the narrative suggests that the other six people knew what to do after the initial proposition. This also fulfills an internal emotional reward relating to group power. Until that is the police arrive at the scene and the young person who presented this narrative disassociated himself from his peers by escaping from the scene. Avoiding arrest was as thrilling as the fire setting; he reflected that he was "buzzing" because he did not get caught. This part of the narrative also serves to elevate his status among the group, as the only person who was skilled enough to avoid arrest.

Any program aiming to support the young person in Box 5.3 needs to take account of his role within his peer group. The initial fire setting was for fun, but it was also a group activity to affirm group behavior. The scale of the fire and the police response made the incident more appealing to this young person. There are also extenuating risk factors associated with arson. One study found that frequent fire starters had an elevated risk of substance use and that the severity of the fire was associated with increased psychological risks (MacKay et al., 2009). The authors recommended that any interventions should include support for substance use addiction and mental illness.

Breaking into an Abandoned Building/Building Site

For the young person in Box 5.4, the incident was literally a game. He described how his group were playing a game in the park when they saw the building site and decided to enter it, initially to see if they could get a security guard to chase them (Ashton & Bussu, 2020). This was not the first time that they had broken into a building site and either instigated a chase or climbed up a crane. His comment that it was someone else's idea and that on this occasion he acted as a lookout by the fence is a reminder that co-offending roles can be static, even within the same group (Uhnoo, 2016). The items that were stolen were of no consequence to the group and so were secondary to the excitement of breaking into the site. As with the narrative in Box 5.3, escaping the police and the following days became a part of the thrill of the main activity.

BOX 5.4 STUDY C: CASE STUDY OF BREAKING INTO A BUILDING SITE

"[We were] pissing about. We was in the [shopping centre] getting chasers because you don't even have to do anything to get chased in there you just stand there in there in a group and you get chased after by security so we were just pissing about in there for a bit. Then we went to a park and played manhunt then we thought oh there's a construction site in there, let's go climb in there, see if we get chased. … It wasn't mine [idea]. It was one of my mates. So we all just did it because it was funny.

There was this big box that some security guard's in so just like throw stones at the door of it and wait for them to come out and then run out. It was funny. … I didn't actually climb the crane on this time. They [friends] climbed up the crane and as they came down there was a couple of things, a sledgehammer, a hammer, a walkie talkie, all this shit. So they just grabbed that on impulse obviously. I've just been stood on the other side of the fence waiting for them, and they just threw it over and I was like oh what's this then, just grab it and run and I was like sweet.

A PCSO came onto the park with a flashlight, so we all bolted and then there was one of them big TAU [Tactical Armed Unit] vans waiting on the other side. So we was like shit and all dashed in different directions and then met up on the main road just off [place] and ended up all going home and then we went out the next day and just started pissing about. It was a mad couple of days. ... I was just laughing. I was a bit paranoid that when someone knocked on the door because nobody knocks on my door but someone knocked on my door that day but no, it wasn't anyone. But then a few days later three of my mates came to my door in the middle of the day. Someone's grassed [told] on us boys, blah, blah, blah. [Boy's] mum, yeah, my mate's mum came to the door the night of that day and was just asking me about it and asking me where all the shit was and I was like I don't know. But we ended up getting it all back to them".

(15 years old. Other offenses included fighting, arson, and criminal damage)

A logical way to counteract thrill-seeking behaviors as described in this case study would be to find alternative legal activities for the young person to take part in. The group of peers encouraged each other, and that the incident was seen as part of a game. However, it is also necessary to consider other offenses that a young person is involved and the motivations for types of offenses (Ashton & Bussu, 2022). For example, all the offenses that were self-reported by the young person in Box 5.4 were expressive or thrill seeking. This is different from the young person who described the burning down of an abandoned house who was involved with the use of serious violence, including violent income generating offenses.

It is also possible that the people within a group experience an offense differently. This can be partly down to individual differences and their motivations for being involved. Another person from Study C described breaking into a disused pool hall with friends and subsequently committing criminal damage after some of the group began to throw glasses at each other (Ashton & Bussu, 2020). His aim was to enter the building to "chill" and play pool. He reported that

We was like just chilling and then just get the odd person who was just being a dickhead and then just threw something ... I don't know, it was just like, it's just chilling with my mates, chilling having a good time and that, didn't really think nothing of it.

This incident acts as a reminder that experiences of the same offense can be different for each participant. It also shows how an individual can control the outcome of a group activity and that other members may be powerless to intervene. In this case only one of the young people was taken to the police station; the person sharing his narrative said that he thought it was because he had been carrying a weapon. This case demonstrates a lack of group unity and motivation and highlights the potential risks that one person (carrying a weapon and behaving impulsively) can pose to a group of friends.

Joyriding

Joyriding is taking a vehicle without consent and using it for the pleasure of driving around. Researchers have found that joyriding often involves driving expensive and fast cars to impress others (Kellet & Gross, 2006). In this sense young people can increase their social status by impressing their peers.

BOX 5.5 STUDY C: CASE STUDY OF THEFT OF A MOTOR VEHICLE

I really like motorbikes. I was just walking and seen the bike in the car park, and then the guy was going in the house, so – just took the locks off it, took it, started it, and then, about three in the morning, was driving, and then – you know, the ANPRs [automatic number plate recognition]. One of them was chasing behind me, and then, like, nudged me, and that was it. ... That's just what we do. That's what I do.

(16 years old)

Given its prevalence among adolescents, there has been comparatively little interest in motor vehicle theft. Nevertheless, researchers have identified different typologies including the need for transportation, recreation (fun, social status), and income generation (Dhami, 2008). However, studies rarely distinguish between the type of motor vehicle that is taken. Data from Study B indicated that there was a progression that aligned with a change of motivation for vehicle theft. A typical sequence of arrests for the 41% of solo offenders and 68% of co-offenders who were associated with this activity was as follows (Figure 6.1):

Stage 1 – theft of bicycles from the street and then out buildings
Stage 2 – opportunistic theft of a motorcycle
Stage 3 – breaking into an outbuilding to steal a motorcycle
Stage 4 – theft of a car for joyriding
Stage 5 – theft of a motorbike or car for resale locally
Stage 6 – involvement in organized car theft

Not all young people reached stages 5 and 6. However, the offense was clustered with other income-generating offenses, including burglary and theft for both the young people in Study B subsample (Figure 1.1) and total sample (Ashton et al., 2021). This typology will be discussed further in Chapter 6.

For the self-reported offending in Study A 34% of the sample reported having stolen a motor vehicle was joyriding. Furthermore, the two crimes shared very similar coordinates on the SSA plot, together with arson (Figure 1.2) and were linked to thrill-seeking behaviors. The case study in Box 5.5, although from a different sample, illustrates the motivation and behavior of a young person at stage 2 of motor vehicle theft. His accomplice is irrelevant and unimportant. His principal motivation is clear, and the behavior was a common event for him. Removing locks from a bike requires some skill and typically in the initial stages young people self-report or are arrested with a more experienced co-offender. It is then common for individuals to take a bike for their own sense of pleasure. Stealing a car can be more group oriented. The young person who stole the car in case study (Box 1.11) shared his acquisition with his friends and in this sense gained social credibility and status with his peers.

It is worth noting that joyriding has been associated with addictive behaviors. A study of convicted joyriders aged 15 to 21 years from the UK found that some young people made the analogy between joyriding and drug use and that many had been unable to stop their behavior (Kellet & Gross, 2006). The researchers stressed that their sample was drawn from incarcerated young people and so those who were arguably the most prolific. However, possible behavioral dependency should be considered so that young people can be appropriately supported. Researchers who identified this problem suggest using Prochaska and DiClemente's (1986) Stages of Change Model (Kellett & Gross, 2006). This model will be familiar to many practitioners and posits that individuals move through six stages of change: precontemplation, contemplation, preparation/determination to change, action, relapse, maintenance, and termination. Although the stages are a cycle, people with an addiction or problem behavior can of course exit and reenter at any stage in the process.

Hate Crimes

Levin and McDevitt (1993) categorized hate crimes in the United States into three motivations: thrill seeking, defensive (protecting something), and mission (against a particular group). McDevitt and colleagues (2002) added a fourth motivation of retaliation. The details of hate-related arrests in Study B indicate that the 10% of the total sample (Ashton et al., 2021),

27% of solo offenders (Figure 1.1), and 50% of co-offenders (Figure 1.5) in the subsample fell into the excitement or retaliatory categories. Most cases with a hate element were associated with a common assault. The majority were reactive, so race became the focus of a response. An example of this from the arrest records was a young person and his friends who racially harassed a shop keeper after an earlier dispute. There is another example of a young person targeting strangers because of their racialized identity, their age, or because they were disabled. His victims were hit, spat on, and verbally abused without any warning or prior interaction, thus falling into Levin and McDevitt's first category of offenders of thrill-seeking offenders.

When considered with other offenses hate crimes were clustered with more serious offenses for the Study B total sample (Ashton et al., 2021) and subsample (Figure 1.1). This does not mean that hate-related offenses were part of involvement with organized crimes but rather those young people who had an arrest for this category of offense went on to become involved in instrumental violence. There could be several explanations for this observation. First, if associated with thrill seeking, perpetrators might be higher risk takers and so more open to involvement with higher levels of criminality. Second, young people who are gang-involved and who commit violent offenses score higher on callous and unemotional traits (Ashton & Ioannou, 2022). Third, in thrill crimes offenders seek excitement and power (McDevitt et al., 2002). It is possible that initial involvement with a criminal group offers the same emotional reward.

Research has indicated that thrill seekers are likely to be part of a group, have no history with their victim, have little commitment to their bias, and that deterrence is likely to work as an intervention (McDevitt et al., 2002). The same study showed that retaliatory offenders are typically alone, often have no history with the offender, a moderate commitment to bias, and are unlikely to be deterred. The lack of history with the offender can be explained by a retaliation against a perceived group of people. In the case of the young people in Study B, race became an element in a reactive response to an individual. A key part of any program to counter hate offending is the level of strength of their bias. McDevitt and colleagues (2002, Table 3) examined how open to change young hate crime offenders were depending on their role. They identified four positions for those involved in thrill-motivated offenses. The "leader". The "fellow traveler" who actively or hesitantly participates. The "unwilling participant" who is not active but does not attempt to stop the offense. The "hero", who attempts to stop the incident. Retaliatory offenses had the same actors with the absence of the leader role. Leaders and fellow travelers were unlikely to change. Unwilling participants were moderately amenable to change, and those fulfilling the hero role were highly amenable to change. Identifying the motivation and the role of a young person in a crime with a hate element is crucial for successfully treating their bias. However, caution is necessary. The narrative roles in criminal action approach that was described in Chapter 1 (Canter & Youngs, 2009; Youngs & Canter, 2012) show that even for behaviors with the same motivation, individuals reveal different roles.

Summary and Implications for Practice

Although sensation or thrill-seeking behaviors generally occur in groups and young people often cite boredom as their motivation, these activities fulfill other purposes. Social and group bonding is one outcome. Some peer groups acted in unity. However, young people also described an individual in their group who escalated an incident, for example, by stealing something or committing criminal damage. It is therefore crucial to understand the role that a young person played within their group activity. As with other crime motivations, sensory offending is dynamic as seen by the progression of joyriding. Hate crimes, which can be thrill-seeking behavior, can also make a young person vulnerable to exploitation by extremist groups at a later stage. With regard to behavioral programs, although finding an alternative and legal sensory activity may assist with young people in early adolescence, the reasons for taking part in thrill seeking offenses can require more complex interventions and take consideration of the influence of peers or a group.

References

Ashton, S. A., & Bussu, A. (2020). Peer groups, street gangs and organised crime in the narratives of adolescent male offenders. *Journal of Criminal Psychology, 10*(4), 277–292.

Ashton, S. A., & Ioannou, M. (2022). The relationship between gang membership and psychological risks to offending desistance in a sample of adolescent and young adult males. *Journal of Gang Research, 29*(2), 1–25.

Ashton, S. A., Valentine, M., & Chan, B. (2021). Differentiating categories of violent adolescent offending and the associated risks in police and youth offending service records. *International Journal of Offender Therapy and Comparative Criminology*.

Ashton, S.-A., & Ward, J. (2022). Bridging the gap between criminal psychology and frontline youthwork: A case study in programme development and evaluation. *Assessment and Development Matters, 14*(4), 15–20.

Becker, G. S. (2000). Crime and punishment: An economic approach. In N.G. Fielding, A. Clarke, & R. Witt (Eds.), *Economic Dimensions of Crime* (pp. 13–68). Palgrave Macmillan.

Burt, C. H., & Simons, R. L. (2013). Self-control, thrill seeking, and crime: Motivation matters. *Criminal Justice and Behavior, 40*(11), 1326–1348.

Canter, D. V., & Youngs, D. (2009). *Investigative psychology: Offender profiling and the analysis of criminal action.* John Wiley & Sons.

Cukrowicz, K. C., Taylor, J., Schatschneider, C., & Iacono, W. G. (2006). Personality differences in children and adolescents with attention-deficit/hyperactivity disorder, conduct disorder, and controls. *Journal of Child Psychology and Psychiatry, 47*(2), 151–159.

Dhami, M. K. (2008). Youth auto theft: A survey of a general population of Canadian youth. *Canadian Journal of Criminology and Criminal Justice, 50*(2), 187–209.

Farrington, D. P., Loeber, R., Jolliffe, D., & Pardini, D. A. (2008). Promotive and risk processes at Dierent life stages. In R. Loeber, D.P. Farrington, M. Stouthamer-Loeber, & H. Rasking White (Eds.), *Violence and serious theft* (pp. 182–242). Routledge.

Katz, J. (1988). *Seductions of crime: Moral and sensual attractions in doing evil.* Basic Books.

Kellett, S., & Gross, H. (2006). Addicted to joyriding? An exploration of young offenders' accounts of their car crime. *Psychology, Crime and Law, 12*(1), 39–59.

Levin, J., & McDevitt, J. (1993). The law. In J. Levin & J. McDevitt (Eds.), *Hate crimes* (pp. 179–203). Springer.

MacKay, S., Paglia-Boak, A., Henderson, J., Marton, P., & Adlaf, E. (2009). Epidemiology of firesetting in adolescents: Mental health and substance use correlates. *Journal of Child Psychology and Psychiatry, 50*(10), 1282–1290.

McDevitt, J., Levin, J., & Bennett, S. (2002). Hate crime offenders: An expanded typology. *Journal of Social Issues, 58*(2), 303–317.

Moffitt, T. E. (1993). The neuropsychology of conduct disorder. *Development and Psychopathology, 5*(1–2), 135–151.

Pfefferbaum, B., & Wood, P. B. (1994). Self-report study of impulsive and delinquent behavior in college students. *Journal of Adolescent Health, 15*(4), 295–302.

Putniņš, A. L. (2010). An exploratory study of young offenders' self-reported reasons for offending. *Journal of Forensic Psychiatry and Psychology, 21*(6), 950–965.

Reiss, A. J. (1986). Co-offender influences on criminal careers. In A. Blumstein, J. Cohen, J. A. Roth & C. A. Visher (Eds.), *Criminal careers and "career criminals" (2).* Washington, DC: National Academy Press.

Tajfel, H., & Turner, J. C. (1982). Social psychology of intergroup relations. *Annual Review of Psychology, 33*(1), 1–39.

Uhnoo, S. (2016). Starting a fire together: The dynamics of co-offending in juvenile arson. *European Journal of Criminology, 13*(3), 315–331.

Warr, M. (1996). Organization and instigation in delinquent groups. *Criminology, 34*(1), 11–37.

Warr, M. (2002). *Companions in crime: The social aspects of criminal conduct.* Cambridge University Press.

Youngs, D. (2006). How does crime pay? The differentiation of criminal specialisms by fundamental incentive. *Journal of Investigative Psychology and Offender Profiling, 3*(1), 1–19.

Youngs, D., & Canter, D. V. (2012). Narrative roles in criminal action: An integrative framework for differentiating offenders. *Legal and Criminological Psychology, 17*(2), 233–249.

Zuckerman, M., & Aluja, A. (2015). Measures of sensation seeking. In G.J. Boyle, D.H. Saklofske, & G. Matthews (Eds.), *Measures of personality and social psychological constructs* (pp. 352–380). Academic Press.

6 Acquisitive Offending

Early Income-generating Offenses

BOX 6.1 STUDY C: CASE STUDY OF IMPROMPTU SHOPLIFTING

Me and my mates –I think it was four of us – went behind – 'cause there was, like, a centre, a shopping centre near where I live, it has [small supermarkets] all shops like that, we went behind it, like, where all the – where they keep all the stuff behind it, and we took a load of things out of the back of there, and then we all got in trouble, at school and with the police. We were on the skate park, just sitting on one of the ramps, and then we all thought we were, like, hungry and thirsty, and we all had no money, so we thought we'd do that. Stupid idea. I said "How about we go and get something from a shop", then everyone said "We have no money", and I said, "Exactly, let's just go and get some things". We grabbed a load of things, and started going, and someone came running out, so, like, we all started running and that. It sounds a bit weird, it's not a good thing, but I had kind of like adrenalin to that and I was going, like, not stopping running, yeah. Before we put our hoods up there was a camera before us and they saw us go off and down, like, down that road near it. Yeah, that was how we were caught. (12 years old)

Shoplifting is typically an early offense and often the only criminal act on a young person's timeline. In Study A 62% of young people self-reported shoplifting and 57% said that they had handled stolen goods. These two activities had a relationship to selling cannabis (41%) and formed the first

DOI: 10.4324/9781003255697-7

stage of income-generating offenses (Figure 1.2). Case study Box 6.1 is typical of shoplifting in early adolescence in all three studies. A combination of needing something and hanging out with friends, when one of the groups suggests stealing smaller items for immediate consumption or use. This participant had shoplifted previously and so knew to try and hide his identity, even though on this occasion he failed to do so. His other self-reported activities were smoking cannabis, criminal damage (slashing car tires and arson), and fighting.

BOX 6.2 STUDY C: CASE STUDY OF PLANNED SHOPLIFTING

Okay well it was just those days, any other day after school, a shop down the road – we go into that shop, we went to the shop, there was me and two other people, one of them one of my closest mates at the time, and a new person I wasn't that close with. We walked in and as… no we didn't walk in, we walked over, as we were walking over we talked about what we were going to do, how we were doing it, and then we went in, did it and walked out. It was either mine or my closest mate's idea because at the time I was the man with a plan. Each of us just went upstairs and just started grabbing things. Like there wasn't a specific role at that time but say it was a bit bigger, then each person would have a specific thing to do. Well at that place where we did it, we did it more than once, we stole alcohol, and then either drank it or sold it. I'd tell one person to go and wait in the toilets, I'd get what I was getting, I'd go to the toilets and then as far as everyone else was seeing, me and that person don't know each other, so…

[There was] the person that I was close with whose idea it may also have been, waiting in the toilets, she was a girl, and she had a bag. If she wasn't there then there'd be a person with a backpack, but one time we just ran out the fire exit. [We got] a bit of a buzz, adrenalin running, blowing off a bit of steam, even more so when we drank it. I overthink things a lot, pretty much everything, so it sort of helps, man with the plan, always thinking – like some would say this is my idea, I take the idea and make sure that it actually works. I'll take myself aside for a couple of minutes, think about it, and then I'll just turn around and go, "Right, here's what we're doing" and then we just do it. (16 years old)

Theft and Burglary

As with other offense categories, there are different motivations for shoplifting and categories of shoplifter (Krasnovsky & Lane, 1998). These are hard to determine from individual arrest records (Study B). However, it is possible to determine patterns of behavior, some of which are relevant to later involvement in instrumental violent offending. Like adults, one category of adolescent shoplifter offends for acquisitive reasons for retail theft (Cox et al., 1990). Others shoplift for sensory or thrill seeking reasons (Zuckerman, 1979). The case study in Box 6.2 shows both motivations being fulfilled. The young person described how shoplifting activities were carefully planned with roles assigned for larger-scale offenses. Describing himself as a "man with a plan" he prided himself on his ability to operationalize other people's ideas. This incident served the purpose of obtaining items for resale and sensory offending (the thrill of the activity and the access to alcohol). In the arrest data it is possible to see the initial skill transfer and learning among peer groups, siblings, or parent. In the case of Study B arrests, shoplifting was considered with theft as an overall category and was a common early offense for those who progressed to other income-generating crimes such as burglary.

Arrest data indicated two distinct groups of early-to-mid-adolescent offenders. Some, like the example in Box 6.2, only commit nonviolent income-generating offenses. Others intersperse income generating with expressive violence; the data indicate that it is this latter category that are most likely to continue to the next stage of income generating with the use of violence. The planning and skill exchange for some cases of shoplifting are transferable to offenses against people.

BOX 6.3 STUDY C: CASE STUDY OF THEFT

I was on work experience. Yeah, and they had a – I was working in the shed, there's, like, a safe, so I kind of planned this – I did work experience for a week, and I remember in the afternoon, when you go to the till, there's this, like, a safe key, so one day I took the safe key, and opened the safe, and no one was about, and there was some money in there, so I decided to take some, but I didn't think it was a lot, but then, it was, like, a couple of days in, and I put some money in the pillow – in my pillow – and then my dad found it, and then – think it was, rough amount – rough amount was eight - one thousand eight hundred. with the money I went to [shop], it's a gaming shop. So I went in there and got an Apple watch and AirPods. (16 years old. Other offenses theft and shoplifting.)

Burglary

Burglary is legally defined as entering a building by trespass and attempting/ stealing something from the property. In England and Wales, the crime can also include committing grievous bodily harm against a person. In police reports it can be difficult to differentiate immediately between the burglary of domestic and business properties easily from the data. Cromwell (1994) identified that adolescent burglars learn from more experienced and older criminals with 77% of his sample reported committing a burglary with an older friend of relative. This was supported by the arrest data from Study B for the subsample, which demonstrated that burglary was associated with an arrest with a co-offender who was five to ten years older than the adolescent (Figure 1.5). However, when the total sample for Study B was considered an older relative with a criminal record did not predict an arrest for burglary. A logistic regression analysis found that three of the independent variables made a unique statistically significant contribution to the model to predict an arrest for burglary: arrest with an older offender with an odds ratio of 3.29, theft of a motor vehicle with an odds ratio of 0.23, and total number of arrests with an odds ratio of 1.01. An arrest with an older offender was therefore the strongest predictor in the model; young people who were arrested with an older co-offender were three times more likely to have an arrest for burglary. Having a family member with a criminal record did not contribute to the model.

The police data for Study B total sample indicated that 34% had been arrested for burglary (Ashton et al., 2021); these ranged from burglary of a shed to house break-ins. In contrast 50% of the subsample had been arrested for burglary alone and 82% with co-offenders, and there was a clear progression from burglarizing out-buildings to houses. Furthermore, when members of the subsample were arrested for multiple burglaries, these were associated with car thefts, so-called car key burglaries (see next section).

In the self-reported data for Study A, 27% of the young people said that they had broken into a building to steal something (Figure 1.2). The most common type of offense was breaking into an abandoned building and theft (Box 6.4). The young person in this case study was aware of the different charges depending on the status of the building. He was also savvy enough not to take any items himself in case they were caught. Although young people can initially find burglary thrilling (Katz, 1988), the crime soon progresses to income generating. In the initial stages of their "training" young people who are learning from an older offender are often only permitted small financial or material rewards. When they can take more or as they learn to be more autonomous burglars there remains the problem of converting items to cash (Cromwell, 1994). In some areas criminal or family networks make it easy for this process to occur. Handling stolen goods appeared with different offenses in Studies A and B. In Study A this was related to other early income-generating offenses (shoplifting and selling cannabis). In Study B subsample it was associated with more serious violent income-generating activities. This can be explained by the difference in ages between the two samples. The Study B subsample had reached late adolescence and had a wider criminal network. In regard to Cromwell's (1994) findings, it is worth considering that in 2022 some environments enable young people to obtain experience in handling stolen goods early in their lives. For example, 57% of the Study A sample self-reported selling stolen items. There may therefore be temporal, regional, or national differences in behaviors and offending opportunities.

In all three studies burglary was associated with the progression to more serious and violent income-generating offenses. It was also associated with higher numbers of arrests. This supports prior research on adult burglars, which found that 91% of perpetrators had committed at least three other offenses (Fox et al., 2020). The same researchers identified different types of burglar, largely depending on their skills and the associated target focus. Young people are still dynamic in terms of their offending styles and knowledge. Those with early onset (7 to 14 years of age) demonstrate a greater offending variety than adolescent or adult starters (Fox et al., 2020). In this respect burglary on a young person's timeline should be a concern for those supporting them and is also an indication of criminal exploitation.

BOX 6.4 STUDY C: CASE STUDY OF BREAKING INTO AN ABANDONED BUILDING AND THEFT

The building hadn't been refurnished or anything so everything was still in there and the shutters were down and we went inside and looked through the whole thing. We found a safe, we broke inside it with a crow bar, found some jewelry at the bottom of it and then we left, and when we left the building the police caught both of us but my mate got caught with something on him and I had nothing on me because I didn't want to take anything. We got, we lifted up the shutters, we walked, well we climbed under it and it was like a reception type thing, it didn't have much furniture in it at the bottom floor but we obviously had a lot of adrenaline going through us and stuff so we was pretty scared so instantly from that floor we didn't want to stay there, we sprinted up the stairs and got on to the second floor and seen loads of mattresses piled up on top of each other and we thought well they must have loads of stuff in here still. We went up to the next floor and that was couches and living room stuff and then we went up to the next floor and it was beds and then it was offices on the next. So that's when we knew, oh there might be a bit of money in here. We went around and there were quite a few safes that were old and rusty but this one was the one that looked the easiest to get in to and like it was not old enough and you could actually break into it. Literally after a couple of pulls of a crowbar and a couple of whacks of the metal at the top casing it come off and we had the things inside of it, but ...

I thought I was getting done for trespassing, but I thought if they found like anything on any of us that it goes from trespassing to a different type of charge. It goes from trespassing to like, robbing, theft because the building, we didn't know that it was private. We thought that it was abandoned not private. But the police said to us, why are you in a private building when they grabbed us so instantly I thought shhh, that's classed as theft. But after happened and I had a bit of like confrontation with them, every time I see them I just thought whatever and every time I had a chase off them, it wasn't adrenaline sprint it was calmly thinking how do you get away from them. (15 years old. Other offenses include robbery with a weapon, burglary, theft, sold cannabis, shoplifted, handled stolen goods, carried a weapon, fighting, assault, criminal damage, arson, driven under the influence of drugs, daily cannabis use.)

Organized Theft of Motor Vehicles

Researchers have called upon police forces to differentiating between car key burglary and regular domestic burglary (Allcock et al., 2011; Shaw et al., 2010). Car key theft occurs at night and is typically in more affluent neighborhoods (Shaw et al., 2010). It therefore requires young people who can be out late at night and, if out of their immediate area, transport. There were two cases in the Study B subsample where individuals had been arrested for keyless car theft as part of an organized criminal group. In general people who commit car key burglaries tend to have convictions for vehicle theft, whereas those who are convicted of general domestic burglary are more likely to have committed shoplifting offenses in the past (Chapman et al., 2012). This is also true of adolescents. Study A theft of a motor vehicle and joyriding preempted burglary. In Study B subsample (Figure 1.1) theft of a motor vehicle was in the same region of the plot as burglary, which accords with its contribution to the regression model to predict burglary. In this cohort 41% of the young people had stolen a vehicle alone and

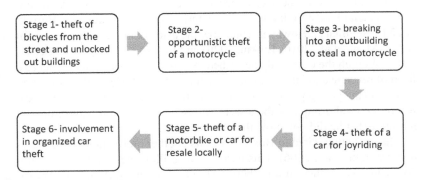

Figure 6.1 Stages of motor vehicle theft

68% with co-offenders. As noted in Chapter 5, theft of motor vehicles can progress from thrill-seeking and joyriding motivations to stealing items for resale (Figure 6.1). Those young people who have the skills to steal cars to sell them on to their local networks are more likely to come to the attention of older offenders who have connections with drug dealing, street-level crimes, and ultimately more organized criminal groups. Distinguishing between car theft for fun and income generating is important, because this will ultimately impact the appropriate focus of any intervention.

Robbery

In the UK robbery is defined as a violent crime involving use of force (see Burrell, 2022 for definitions and discussion). As one of the young people in Study C pointed out, regarding sentencing (Chapter 5), robbery can be committed against a person or a business. For the purposes of this publication robbery falls into the personal category and can involve a weapon or the threat of physical violence from a group (Burrell, 2022; Porter & Alison, 2006). Research has found that most robberies are committed by two or more offenders (Burrell et al., 2012). This was supported by the Study B subsample which found that 27% had committed robbery alone (Figure 1.1) compared to 68% with a co-offender; co-offenders often included someone five to ten years older on a young person's overall arrest record (Figure 1.5). However, in the arrest records it was unusual for repeat co-arrestees. As with other offense categories people fulfill different roles in the commissioning of a robbery. For the Study A cohort robbery was associated with more serious income-generating offenses such as burglary, possession with intent to supply class A drugs, and carjacking. Of this sample, 21% had committed a robbery with a weapon and 33% without.

Motivations for robbery can vary and include financial rewards to support financial hardship, the need for material goods, or drugs (see Burrell, 2022 for summary). However, young people also commit robbery for social status (Monk et al., 2010; Tonkin, 2020) and for excitement (Harding et al., 2019). As with the case study described in Box 4.1 robbery can also act as a form of revenge and intimidation (Brookman et al., 2007). In the case study (Box 4.1) the young person robbed the victim because he would not reveal where the rival group members were; although it seems probable from the narrative that he did not know their whereabouts.

The case study cited in Box 6.5 reveals another motivation for robbery-debt (Wright et al., 2006). This narrative also illustrates the influence of a dominant accomplice in a robbery (Alarid et al., 2009; Ashton & Bussu, 2020), and how the presence of others can obviate the need for a weapon. The young people in Study A were asked about weapon use; 21% reported committing a robbery with a weapon and 33% without. The arrest data from Study B showed that group robberies without a weapon typically occurred earlier in a trajectory and that young people progressed to solo robberies with a weapon. The narrative described in Box 1.3 was an example of a pair who planned street robberies in the sense that they carried weapons to use when an opportunity arose. This pair was also accomplished and familiar with each other's way of operating to the extent that the young person described the decision to commit this offense as instantaneous (Ashton & Bussu, 2020). The young person gained social capital by committing the robbery and carjacking (see Chapter 7). This phenomenon is also relevant for informal peer group accomplice selection as a form of social exchange (Ashton & Bussu, 2020; Weerman, 2003). Although traditionally associated with gang involvement (Harding et al., 2019), the occurrences of robbery in all three studies for the present publication were not directly associated with gang membership. Rather, they were supplementary activities that served the purposes of generating personal income or enhanced antisocial status.

What was clear from the self-reported data and the arrest records in Studies A and B was that the appearance of robbery on a young person's timeline was indicative of a heightened risk of involvement with organized criminal groups. This relationship is not straightforward. The arrest data and the narratives from Study C indicate that robbery is not something that those involved with criminal groups and the sale of class A drugs undertake as part of their group's activities (Ashton & Bussu, 2022). Rather, this was an additional income-generating opportunity that was often executed alone or with peers from outside of the criminal group. This can be explained by membership of multiple criminal groups (peers, street gangs, and organized; Ashton & Bussu, 2020).

BOX 6.5 STUDY C: CASE STUDY OF ROBBERY

I don't really get involved in much no more, but I used to get involved in, like, you know, shooting, like, weed, stuff like that, and more or less, like, do you know, like, I've robbed a few people, but after that, you started – obviously, but you started feeling like, "Oh shit, I feel bad for this", but you got made to do it, 'cause it was, like, if you didn't do it – it was more or less being in them situations, it wasn't your – what you wanted to do – what you was made to do, you was forced to do it, basically, and it was just – it was like, well – like when once, like, it was some kid who owed money to me and my mate, I was just like, "No, just leave it" – he was "If you don't get the money I'll just punch him right in his face." [unclear, 11.09] "we should be dealing with it mate" – "Fuck off, I need money now." –"All right then, we'll find him, We'll speak to him." Turned up, I went, "Listen, not being funny, need the money." Kid went "You're not getting your fucking money." So I went "Wait a minute, I mean, you owe us money, you've just cost us money, and that's not how things go down, mate." I went, "Don't, like, take the piss." And then my mate straight away smacked him, and I went "What are you doing?" He went, "Grab the phone." "What do you mean, grab the phone?" "Just grab the phone" – 'cause his phone's fell out of his pocket, this kid's. I went "Oh, for fuck's sake", like that, grabbed the phone, and then I went to actually give it the kid back, and my mate grabbed it off me, went "Fuck off", I went, "What do you mean?" "Fuck off, I'm having this phone now, and I'm taking it." "All right, sweet then." And then he's – and then the kid was like, "Oi, have this instead of your money", give us a watch, I was like – I looked at it, I was like, "This watch is about two ton, mate, you don't owe us that, you owe us about thirty quid', and he was like, "No, no, let's do that" – obviously took it, 'cause he was like, "We've got our money back now", but after it, I was like, "That was a bit unnecessary, that, taking his phone." My mate was like, "Oh, go fuck, he owed us money, he's took the piss" – I was like, "Yeah, he's took piss, but you don't need to take his fucking phone, he's just give us a watch that's worth two ton" – he was like, "I don't give a fuck, I want his phone, he's not ringing me again, is he" – I was like, "Right then". (16 years old. Other offenses include an assault, criminal damage, robbery, fighting, selling class A and B drugs, daily cannabis use.)

Summary and Implications for Practice

All the income-generating offenses in this chapter rely on the learning and use of skills to acquire something of value. Together they represent a change in motivation, and it is this development that leaves young people open to an enhanced risk of criminal exploitation by adults. Involvement in car key burglaries could indicate a shift from joyriding to theft for resale either on a local level or as part of a more organized network. Although typically nonviolent in nature, other behaviors should be considered when assessing the risk posed by burglary and theft of a motor vehicle offenses on a young person's timeline.

Robbery is the culmination of violent and acquisitive behaviors. There are different motivations for committing a robbery (debt collection, thrill seeking, status enhancement, revenge, income). Although often undertaken in groups, the data from all three studies suggest that the offense is not necessarily part of organized criminal activities during adolescence. Rather, robbery is an activity that adolescents who exhibit increased violence and risk take part in as an opportunity arises.

References

Alarid, L. F., Burton Jr., V. S., & Hochstetler, A. L. (2009). Group and solo robberies: Do accomplices shape criminal form? *Journal of Criminal Justice, 37*(1), 1–9.

Allcock, E., Bond, J. W., & Smith, L. L. (2011). An investigation into the crime scene characteristics that differentiate a car key burglary from a regular domestic burglary. *International Journal of Police Science and Management, 13*(4), 275–285.

Ashton, S. A., & Bussu, A. (2020). Peer groups, street gangs and organised crime in the narratives of adolescent male offenders. *Journal of Criminal Psychology, 10*(4), 277–292.

Ashton, S. A., & Bussu, A. (2022). The social dynamics of adolescent co-offending. *Youth Justice, 17*(3).

Ashton, S. A., Valentine, M., & Chan, B. (2021). Differentiating categories of violent adolescent offending and the associated risks in police and youth offending service records. *International Journal of Offender Therapy and Comparative Criminology.*

Brookman, F., Mullins, C., Bennett, T., & Wright, R. (2007). Gender, motivation and the accomplishment of street robbery in the United Kingdom. *British Journal of Criminology, 47*(6), 861–884.

Burrell, A. (2022). *Robbery*. Palgrave Macmillan.

Burrell, A., Bull, R., & Bond, J. (2012). Linking personal robbery offences using offender behaviour. *Journal of Investigative Psychology and Offender Profiling, 9*(3), 201–222.

Chapman, R., Smith, L. L., & Bond, J. W. (2012). An investigation into the differentiating characteristics between car key burglars and regular burglars. *Journal of Forensic Sciences, 57*(4), 939–945.

Cox, D., Cox, A. D., & Moschis, G. P. (1990). When consumer behavior goes bad: An investigation of adolescent shoplifting. *Journal of Consumer Research, 17*(2), 149–159.

Cromwell, P. (1994). Juvenile burglars. *Juvenile and Family Court Journal, 45*(2), 85–91.

Fox, B., Farrington, D. P., Kapardis, A., & Hambly, O. C. (2020). *Evidence-based offender profiling*. Routledge.

Harding, S., Deuchar, R., Densley, J., & McLean, R. (2019). A typology of street robbery and gang organization: Insights from qualitative research in Scotland. *British Journal of Criminology, 59*(4), 879–897.

Katz, J. (1988). *Seductions of crime: Moral and sensual attractions in doing evil*. Basic Books.

Krasnovsky, T., & Lane, R. C. (1998). Shoplifting: A review of the literature. *Aggression and Violent Behavior, 3*(3), 219–235.

Monk, K. M., Heinonen, J. A., & Eck, J. E. (2010). *Problem-oriented guides for police problem-specific guides series no. 59*. Center for Problem-Oriented Policing. Retrieved September 29, 2022.

Porter, L. E., & Alison, L. J. (2006). Behavioural coherence in group robbery: A circumplex model of offender and victim interactions. *Aggressive Behavior: Official Journal of the International Society for Research on Aggression, 32*(4), 330–342.

Shaw, S. E., Smith, L. L., & Bond, J. W. (2010). Examining the factors that differentiate a car key burglary from a regular domestic burglary. *International Journal of Police Science and Management, 12*(3), 450–459.

Tonkin, M. (2020). The pathway into property crime. In A. Burrell & M. Tonkin (Eds.), *Property crime* (pp. 23–37). Routledge.

Weerman, F. M. (2003). Co-offending as social exchange: Explaining characteristics of co-offending. *British Journal of Criminology, 43*(2), 398–416.

Wright, R., Brookman, F., & Bennett, T. (2006). The foreground dynamics of street robbery in Britain. *British Journal of Criminology, 46*(1), 1–15.

Zuckerman, M. (1979). Sensation seeking and risk taking. In C.E. Izard (Ed.), *Emotions in personality and psychopathology* (pp. 161–197). Springer.

7 Criminal Groups and Exploitation

Narratives

The narrative examples in this chapter come from four young people who took part in Study C and were directly involved with drug selling and trafficking. **Participant 1** (Boxes 7.1, 7.2, 7.5, 7.8, and 7.9) A 17-year-old who was trafficked at the age of 16 for six weeks. His only self-reported offending was for fighting alone. He escaped from the gang when he was arrested. **Participant 2** (Box 7.3; Ashton & Bussu, 2020 listed as Participant 1), a 16-year-old, was involved in class A drug selling and who was trafficked at the age of 15; his involvement with the adult crime group lasted around six months. His self-reported offending included drug selling, fighting, criminal damage, and robbery. He offended alone and with others. He escaped from the gang when he was arrested. **Participant 3** (Boxes 6.5, 7.4, 7.6, and 7.7), a 16-year-old who became involved with an adult criminal group through family crime connections and who sold drugs locally and was exposed to extreme levels of violence from the ages of 15 to 16 years. His self-reported offending included assault, criminal damage, robbery, and fighting. He offended alone and with others. He told the gang that he no longer wanted to be involved with their activities after meeting a new girlfriend. **Participant 4** (Boxes 1.3 and 5.3), a 16-year-old who, at the time of the interview, was still actively involved with street-level gangs and an adult criminal group. Related self-reported activities included street robberies, carjacking, drug dealing, fighting, driven under the influence of drugs, and theft. He was also involved with delinquent peer groups (Box 5.3) and street-level gangs (Box 1.3; Ashton & Bussu, 2020). He offended mostly alone, but also with others.

These four case studies highlight the importance of considering criminal narrative experiences for this category of criminal involvement. Ashton and colleagues (forthcoming) identified that participants 1 and 4 presented as calm professionals, whereas participants 2 and 3 represented depressed

DOI: 10.4324/9781003255697-8

victims in their narratives. Although all four young people had been exploited by adult criminals, the way in which they rationalize their role and motivations for their behaviors requires different behavioral and psychological support.

Gangs, Groups, and Syndicates

Although gang involvement is recognized as an increased risk for involvement with long-term and serious violent crime, criminologists have failed to provide a comprehensive definition for a gang (Bennett & Holloway, 2004). As with any other category of criminal involvement, there are different types of gangs, and even within a single gang the experiences and commitment to that group vary considerably between its members and their level of embeddedness in the group (Pyrooz et al., 2013). Participants for Study C were asked how they would define a gang (Ashton & Bussu, 2020). They were consistently able to identify three types of distinct, but not discreet, categories of adolescent groups with delinquent or criminal behavior central to their identity. Ashton and Bussu (2020) reported the following distinctions. The first group was "peers"; this category is described in Chapter 5 and central to their identity are sensory rewards, involved in chasing, fighting, often with the use of recreational cannabis. The second group was "street gangs", also known as a "pop-up gang"; this group was associated with knife carrying, drug selling, and more fighting with weapons. This group encountered the peer groups, as described in a fight where some of the opposing people had weapons, to the surprise of the young person sharing his narrative (Box 1.5; Ashton & Bussu, 2020). The third category was organized crime group (OCG); all the young people differentiated this group by its purpose of making money. As noted in Chapter 5, membership of these groups was not exclusive; some young people were involved with street gangs and OCGs. These findings replicate McLean's (2018) evolving gang model for Scottish youth. His groups were the recreational stage of "youth street gang" involved in delinquent rather than criminal activities. "Youth crime gang", for who criminality, drugs, and territory are intrinsic to group identity. Finally, the "syndicate" stage, which was no longer territorial, involved adults and with financial rewards central to the group. McLean (2018) found that the core members of the young street gang were most likely to progress to the young crime gang. The main difference between the two sets of research findings is the multiple group membership reported by Ashton and Bussu's (2020) sample; this study also retained the labels used by the participants.

Outside of academia, caution is needed when using terms that relate to gangs. For example, some researchers (Densley, 2013; Hesketh & Robinson,

2019) see drugs as the central driver of street gangs. Holligan et al. (2020) found that most community-level drug dealing in their Scottish sample was undertaken by non-gang-affiliated social dealers operating in friendship networks. In short, there are regional differences within the UK and it is essential to find out how young people define and make sense of gangs in their area. Imposing global or academic definitions risks misunderstanding and misinterpreting youth involvement in delinquent and criminal groups or, worse still, the labeling of young people as "gang involved" (Densley & Pyrooz, 2020; Jacobs, 2009). For this reason, when supporting young people, it would be more helpful to understand the types of activities they are involved with and who their associates are (Cotrell-Boyce, 2013; Bullock & Tilley, 2008). Arrest records can indicate the stage or group with whom a young person is connected, for example, the age of co-arrestees (peers, older friends, or adults who are a generation older).

Although a young person may be involved with a third-tier group (OCG/ Syndicate), their exposure to members is generally controlled by a hierarchy (Densley, 2012, 2014; Holligan et al., 2020). This was referenced by Participant 2 in Study C, who spoke of "big guy ... he might be, like, a mob boss or whatever" (Ashton & Bussu, 2020, Table 2). Participant 4 also recounted how he had received "stripes" [recognition] via a phone call from "an elder who was high-up", after he had gained money after selling the vehicle he had carjacked (Box 1.3). Densley (2012) identified a hierarchal structure of a closed inner circle of associates, elders (17- to 24-year-olds), and younger people (12- to 16-year-olds). The young people in Study C identified an additional level between the inner circle and elders with a status that in between and who were aged in their thirties, for example the man who approached Participant 1 (Box 7.2). Their initial contact with young people was an important part of the stage to impress them, after which time the elders (17- to mid-20-year-olds) took over contact and control. For most young people, the OCG members who they encounter are those who manage or sell drugs on the streets, often older members of street-level gangs (Ashton & Bussu, 2020). In this sense there is an additional level in Densley's hierarchy of OCG membership. This process is visible in police arrest records, and the two levels of elders are typically known to the police.

Pathways to Exploitation

Although there are key behaviors that appear on the timelines of exploited young people such as burglary and robbery (Figure 1.3), there is not a single route to criminal group exploitation. Young people are individuals, and their offense histories prior to being exploited by adult criminal gangs differ according to other psychological and social factors that are present in their lives. The 2011 UK government strategy identified early adverse childhood experiences, parental violence, drugs, school exclusions, conduct disorders, and violent victimization as key risks (HM Government, 2011; see also HM Government, 2020). Additionally, researchers have recognized the role of social deprivation (Cotrell-Boyce, 2013), environmental and social risks (Hesketh, 2019), and a lack of legitimate income-generating opportunities (Hesketh & Robinson, 2019).

Local and regional variations may be found. When the two local areas were considered separately for Study B subsample, a significant correlation in the first area was found between possession of intent to supply class A drugs (as an indication of street-level OCG exposure) and possession of A and B drugs, intent to supply class B drugs, handling stolen goods, vehicle offenses, and burglary. In the second locality possession with intent to supply class A drugs was correlated with the same offenses and the addition arrests of racially aggravated assault, sexual assault, and a public order arrest. Once involved, the stories that young people recount share similarities regarding the methods used to coerce them and the activities that they are involved in. Internationally the reason why young people join a gang is often for protection from neighborhood violence (Melde et al., 2012). However, increased exposure to violence is the reason why people leave. Psychological differences between adolescent gang members and leavers have shown that gang membership is associated with increased risk of trauma and violent offending (Ashton & Ioannou, 2022). However, the "inner narratives" (Canter, 1994) and the role they seem themselves playing within the group could also play a crucial role in supporting them to break away (Ashton et al., forthcoming).

BOX 7.1 STUDY C: CHILD CRIMINAL EXPLOITATION

It was like, they was basically bribing us to do their bidding, 'cause if we – basically, what – my dad turned round to me a few month ago and we was speaking about it, and he said, "Do you realise now – they were using kids – they was using kids because no copper's going to suspect a thirteen-year-old, a fourteen-year-old, to be carrying round a knife or a bleeding – stuff on them to sell" – and when I heard that, I just thought in my head, "Oh my God, that's true" – 'cause police won't look at us, we was just little kids who were dressed in tracksuits and that. (Participant 1, 17 years old)

Participants in Study C described two main pathways to criminal exploitation by so-called organized crime groups (OCGs; Ashton & Bussu, 2020). Both rely on adults identifying vulnerable young people, grooming, psychological conditioning, physical violence, and coercion. The grooming process is traditionally seen as offering incentives in the form of designer goods, physical violence, and debt bondage (Hesketh & Robinson, 2019). The selection process by adult criminals is also an important element in understanding how best to prevent exploitation (Whittaker et al., 2020). Having selected a potential target, the adults tested their victims' abilities with illegal tasks such as holding firearms or drugs, drug preparation and sales, and drug trafficking. They also expose them to high levels of violence and violent offenses. The young people in Study C self-identified factors that had led to their involvement with these groups (Figure 7.1). These included their age, exposure through purchasing and selling drugs for their own use, being out on the street late at night, the lure of income and/or status, and importantly being in a location where the adult criminals operated. Young people reported being either introduced to an adult through peers, older friends, or family members, or being approached by a stranger. The latter phenomenon typically occurred in a context where there were other criminal activities; for example the young person in Box 7.2 described being approached in an area where there were shops selling counterfeit goods.

Entry Point 1

The exploiter asked Participant 1 (Box 7.1) questions to see if he fitted an appropriate profile for exploitation (underage and desire to make money). This is the same approach as young people being approached on the streets by dealers or recruiters. Adults will look for adolescents who are already hanging around on the streets with their friends and will initiate contact. The initial period of grooming may be longer in the second case, but the overall process is the same. The reason that young people are so valuable to adult criminals is that they believe they are less likely to be picked up by the police, and if they are arrested, they are seen to be a disposable resource and can easily be replaced.

BOX 7.2 STUDY C: APPROACHED BY A STRANGER

[At college] I done a level one course, went to a level two and I was still ahead of everyone in my class so I was there for like a month, two maybe, and then I dropped out and then I was approached by someone, said, "Do you want to make a bit of money? and obviously when you come from a background where you're not on a stable income, sometimes you don't have a lot of money, if someone comes to you about money, money is money at the end of the day. You've got to do what you do for money, so I was approached, just basically taken on as someone who do like, got told what to do, basically. So yeah, I was basically someone's runner, running about, drugs and such, stuff like that. It was just, that's when we go back to friends, that's where you don't ... it was just a stranger who made friends and then went from being friends to, "You're doing this for me." That's what it was.

I'd estimate he was about thirties, something like that, so yeah I was approached, he was like, "How are you?" "I'm good.' "Where are you from?" I told him where I'm from, he's like, "How old are you?" and I like told him how old I was at the time, at the time I was sixteen and he was like, "Oh right, you should give me your phone number and we can you know, chat some time." So it was you know like, "Yeah you're a sound person," you don't meet many sound people. Obviously he's not a sound person 'cause he wanted one thing and that's what he got. So yeah time went by, maybe a week or two, speaking to me, "How am I doing?" and he said, "Do you want to earn yourself a bit of money?" and I'm like, "Doing what?" and he's like, "Just taking something somewhere for me," "Like what is it?" and he said, "Nothing important, just take it and I'll give you a bit of money," so obviously it weren't nothing major, apparently in his eyes so he sorted out train tickets, I went up to said place which was [county] from [city] and then I got there and basically I was someone's runner, running around [county] shotting heroin and crack to people. Went on for a bit of a period of time, got arrested, got charged with the drugs basically, but yeah ... I was lucky, he don't know where I live, I don't know who he is, I didn't breathe a word about anything, obviously in my interviews "no comment," nothing like that. (Participant 1, 17 years old)

Entry Point 2 from Street-Level Gangs to Organized Crime Involvement

The second route to exploitation occurs through a known associate. This can be a peer, older friend, or family member who introduces the adult gang member to the target. This route can involve a recruiter "talent"-scouting a young person who is selling drugs for their own use. This process was described by Participant 2 (Box 7.3; Ashton & Bussu, 2020). It is also possible to identify this phenomenon from the arrest records. Figure 1.5 indicated that offences associated with exposure to OCGs (possession with intent to supply class A drugs, access to a firearm, attempted murder) were clustered around a history of an arrest with a non-familial adult who was ten or more years older than the young person. Often the adult was not charged and was released with no further action; where charges did occur, it was typically one of adolescents who was caught with the evidence. The presence of a non-familial adult at the scene of an arrest with a child (irrespective of the nature of that offense) is a strong indicator for criminal exploitation. At the very least it indicates a vulnerability on account of the young people to future OCG exploitation. Peers can also act as mediators for contact with OCGs, which is why the backgrounds of all co-arrestees should be considered when attempting to understand the level of risk associated with a young person.

BOX 7.3 STUDY C: EXPLOITATION AND TRAINING

It was mainly – I started off, like, selling weed for – obviously I don't want to mention names, but quite, you know, quite a high – big family in [town], like, and I was selling it for them, and I was selling the weed and, you know, they handed me a bit of coke and said, You know, try selling that. And I got good at it, you know, I got really good at it, like, selling it and that, I got a really banging line going, probably doing about a grand a day, fifteen grand a day, you know, I was just smashing it for a while. And then one of my mates just said to me, You know, let's try and whip [prepare] it and that, so – All right – I went to [town] to one of my mate's houses, and just went in, he said "This is how you do it, that's how you do it', and that, and I whipped it, and then he went, I'll give this to one of the nitties [addicts], he give it as a tester, he tested it, blew his fucking head off – That's the best gear I've had in a while – so he gave a few samples to his mates and that, and, you know, it kind of went from there, you know, and kind of like started noticing and then got in contact with me and then they came up to see me and that, and I'd – you know, we'd all, like, chill out or go out for a bit of food or something, you know, just kind of getting to know each other a bit and just showing, like, what your skills are, kind of like a job interview, you know what I mean. (Participant 2, 16 years old)

Process and Impact

Participant 2 (Box 7.3) described his exploitation journey as a "job interview" and trial. The initial involvement was through an older friend who had contacts with the OCG. Participant 2 also recounted the abuse that he suffered whereby the person who collected the money would accuse the young person of losing some of the total amount, would physically assault him, and then locate the missing amount. This process is the same as the trauma-coercive bonding that is recognized in child sexual exploitation cases (Sanchez et al., 2019). This research identified four key components in trauma coercive bonding: (1) severe power imbalance; (2) intermittent brutal and seductive behavior; (3) social isolation; (4) perceived inability to escape (Sanchez et al., 2019, Figure 1). The key difference in their model is the centrality of coercion, a trait that the authors state is a key to exploiting adolescents. Although the focus of their research was the sexual exploitation of children and adolescents, the relationship with a criminal adult and the tactics that are described by young people who have been criminally exploited by street-level OCG members is similar, if not the same. How young people changed their view and escaped from their involvement is discussed further below. Family can act as a protective factor for young people who have been coerced and exploited, as reference by Participant 1 in talking to his father about his experiences (Box 7.1).

An additional risk for some young people is family involvement with organized crime (Box 7.4). Some of the young people from Study B subsample were directly involved with parents, uncles/aunts, or older siblings. For others, such as Participant 3 (Ashton & Bussu, 2020), familial criminal involvement was indirect but was a constant presence when he was growing

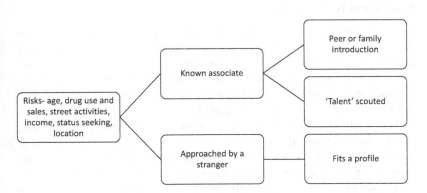

Figure 7.1 Pathways to adolescent involvement with OCGs

up. The strategy of the group that he was involved with was different to that described in Box 7.3. In his case, he was present when firearms were used. In this way he was criminalized by the group and told that he would be sent to prison if he told anyone about his experiences. Ultimately, although his own father had been involved in street-level robberies and violence, the family supported the son when he left the OCG. Perhaps not in a traditional sense, but his father told him that the group had just wanted to exploit him. It is essential, when supporting a young person who has been exploited, to understand which process has put them at risk. This is because the family can act as a protective or a risk factor in criminal exploitation (Aldridge et al., 2012).

BOX 7.4 STUDY C: FAMILY ASSOCIATIONS

My uncle's been, cousins have been, stuff like that, so I get affiliated with that straight away, but mostly for me, we were younger people and then as we started to get a bit older, I'd say, like, 15, like, 14, 15, stuff like that, then we started, like, getting involved in, like, elders, as they call them – older people and they're like, "Yeah, do this, you'll get this much money, we'll get you this" – stuff like that – and I was like, they're treating us, like, with respect and that, so we would treat them with respect, we'd do what they tell us to do and, yeah, that was how it was, basically.

Participant 3, 16 years old (Ashton & Bussu, 2020, p. 283, table 2, quotation 4)

Associated Risk Factors

The professional risk factors that had a significant correlation to an arrest for intent to supply class A drugs for Study B Sample 1 were: risk of drug debt, street gang membership, peer criminal grooming, adult grooming, and victim of bullying. Whereas the program referral risks for Study A (Figure 1.2) indicated an association between a parent in prison or justice involved, and family violence with the selling of class A drugs.

The local neighborhood can increase the risk of exploitation to young people, particularly if this increases exposure to adult criminals (Wood & Alleyne, 2010). For Participant 1, crime was an inevitable occurrence on the estate where he lived, and he distinguished between attitudes to crime by comparing his estate to a more affluent area where crime was not tolerated (Box 7.5).

BOX 7.5 STUDY C: ENVIRONMENTAL RISKS

You're raised up in an area where crime is literally every day normal life, you see it, just, it's not bothering you. Like you might see someone get robbed, you might see someone's bike get stole, you just don't say nothing about … it's just everyday life. Whereas if a middle-class person saw it, it's a big thing, it's a big thing, like you see a lot when you're round areas but there's nothing you can do about it. (Participant 1, 17 years old)

The initial enticement can be the immediate gratification of a substantial income from drug selling. Adult predators play on a broader lack of opportunity and potential to manipulate young people (Whittaker, 2018). However, all the young people in Study C who had been involved with OCGs reported that the money they were initially paid soon ceased. Participant 3 (Box 7.6) mentioned social class several times during his interview and compared himself to families who were in a better financial position. Programs giving young people from socially deprived backgrounds the potential to see how they might have a future career could be an effective way of offering them an alternative pathway. Giving them access to legitimate and successful business owners or professionals from their area would be one way of demonstrating how involvement in crime isn't the only available apprenticeship.

BOX 7.6 STUDY C: DEPRIVATION AND LACK OF OPPORTUNITY

People who I know and stuff like that, we didn't really have no money as kids, we wanted money 'cause we wanted to go out and buy this, buy that, so we was, like, seeing people who were, like, their families have got money, and they was like, they was getting everything they wanted. They was getting life handed to them on a gold plate, basically, silver spoon and everything in their mouth, and we had nothing. We was brought up like a little shit, yeah, you was like rammed it, so basically it was like slums to kids who were getting everything they wanted and that. So we was like, "Well, if we can't get money off our parents and we can't get a job, how are we going to make money?" Be in a gang, stuff like that, so, like, it wasn't really a choice, it's 'cause you need money, it's like – money's dangerous, in my opinion,

> it's horrible, but you need money to live, like, you want to, 'cause you don't want to be like some little poor scruff on the street and people looking at you – "Ha, you got nothing" – and that's what we were like, so I was like, we need to do this, so we can have money. (Participant 3, 16 years old)

Social Rewards

It is not only the promise of financial gain leaves some young people vulnerable to exploitation. Participants (for example Box 7.7) referred to the social rewards that are associated with co-offending adolescents more generally (Warr, 2002). Unfortunately, involvement can jeopardize other healthy relationships with peers and pro-social adults (Williams & Finlay, 2018), thus leading to further isolation and vulnerability. This can partly be explained by criminal social identity theory (Boduszek et al., 2016), which for adults combined an identity crisis, exposure to criminal environment, the need to associate with a criminal group for self-esteem, and a moderating role of psychopathic traits. For adolescents these traits are those present in the previous stages of criminal involvement (lower levels of impulse control, callous responses, and the ability to manipulate peers). Ashton and Ward (2022) found that manipulative traits could be reduced for young people taking part in a targeted intervention.

BOX 7.7 STUDY C: FINANCIAL SOCIAL REWARDS

Yeah, and, like, it's money and most of the time with me as well, it was respect, 'cause, like, if you did something for someone, they'd do something for you, and it was like, if you need backing with this, say someone's starting on you, backing you, even though I don't really need backing. (Participant 3, 16 years old)

Leaving the Gang

Young people who are involved with adult criminal gangs are exposed to considerable psychological and physical harm (Moyle, 2019; Sturrock & Holmes, 2015). Leaving the gang is just the starting point on their desistance journey, and they remain at an elevated level of risk to criminal exploitation, in addition to suffering from psychological trauma from exposure to violence (Ashton & Ioannou, 2022). This can be difficult for young people trying to reconnect with their families and friends after being exploited, as referenced by Participant 1 (Box 7.8).

BOX 7.8 STUDY C: EXPOSURE TO VIOLENCE

It's not nice, you see things you don't wanna see, but just makes you the person who you are, basically, you've just got to get a grip of it, grow up, that's why I'm like when people say to me, "How old are you?" and I describe myself, I think of myself now as more grown up than I should be than any other seventeen year olds, playing out, going McDonalds, doing what they need to, playing video games. I don't see the point of none of that anymore because I'm more mature, I know I'm more mature than anyone else so. (Participant 1, 17 years old)

US studies have found that leaving a gang is the norm, and the average time that people remain a member is between one and two years (Pyrooz, 2013). However, in the UK young people are taught early in the process that their families will come to harm if they tell anyone about their involvement or the activities relating to the group (Box 7.9). For Participants 1 and 2 their connection with the criminal groups who were exploiting them ended after they had been arrested. Participant 2 was threatened if he gave the authorities any information. Participant 3 made the decision to leave his exploiters, who lived locally, after meeting a new girlfriend. He reported that he had told his contacts that he no longer wanted to be involved, and when he had convinced them that if he informed on the group, he would essentially incriminate himself, they accepted this. These stories stress the importance of young people seeing alternative pathways and knowing where to turn for support when they have the courage to leave. The narratives also suggest that an arrest can be a key turning point for a young person, who may be seen as too great a risk by the criminal gang.

**BOX 7.9 STUDY C: LEAVING
THE CRIMINAL GROUP**

A lot goes through your head at the moment, it's just want to get it over and done with 'cause you get yourself stuck into a situation that you can only get out of, basically, but it's hard to get out of, you've got no one to tell, you don't want to tell anyone basically, you can't tell your mum cause what's your mum gonna do, you know she can't come round there just shouting at people, you can't tell the police 'cause that's not what you're brought up to do, you don't go snitching on your own doorstep, basically. (Participant 1, 17 years old)

Summary and Implications for Practice

For some young people there is a clear route from expressive and reactive aggression to violent income-generating offenses, which leaves them vulnerable to criminal exploitation and involvement with drug selling and criminal groups. However, being in an environment where organized criminal groups operate and having a desire to make money presents an equal level of risk. It is possible, indeed the norm, to leave a street gang/organized criminal group. The most common way for this to occur is following an arrest. However, the young person and their family are at risk of retaliation if the criminal groups believe that they have given information to the police. Gang desistance does not automatically mean desistance from crime. Following involvement with adult criminal groups a young person is likely to have suffered psychological trauma and heightened exposure to violence. For many young people, they cannot see a way of leaving a criminal operation. For this reason, access to trained youth workers and/or specialist community focused police officers is crucial.

References

Aldridge, J., Medina-Ariz, J., & Ralphs, R. (2012). Counting gangs: Conceptual and validity problems with the Eurogang definition. In F-A. Esbensen & C.L. Maxson (Eds.), *Youth gangs in international perspective* (pp. 35–51). Springer.

Ashton, S. A., & Bussu, A. (2020). Peer groups, street gangs and organised crime in the narratives of adolescent male offenders. *Journal of Criminal Psychology, 10*(4), 272–292.

Ashton, S. A., & Ioannou, M. (2022). The relationship between gang membership and psychological risks to offending desistance in a sample of adolescent and young adult males. *Journal of Gang Research, 29*(2), 1–25.

Ashton, S. A., Ioannou, M., & Hammond, L. (forthcoming). Applying the criminal narrative roles and emotions to young people who offend in groups.

Ashton, S. A., & Ward, J. (2022). Bridging the gap between criminal psychology and frontline youthwork: A case study in programme development and evaluation. *Assessment and Development Matters, 14*(4), 15–20.

Bennett, T., & Holloway, K. (2004). Gang membership, drugs and crime in the UK. *British Journal of Criminology, 44*(3), 305–323.

Boduszek, D., Dhingra, K., & Debowska, A. (2016). The integrated psychosocial model of criminal social identity (IPM-CSI). *Deviant behavior, 37*(9), 1023–1031.

Bullock, K., & Tilley, N. (2008). Understanding and tackling gang violence. *Crime Prevention and Community Safety, 10*(1), 36–47.

Canter, D. V. (1994). *Criminal shadows: Inside the mind of the serial killer* (pp. 63–69). London: HarperCollins.

Cottrell-Boyce, J. (2013). Ending gang and youth violence: A critique. *Youth Justice, 13*(3), 193–206.

Densley, J. (2013). *How gangs work.* Palgrave Macmillan.

Densley, J. A. (2012). Street gang recruitment: Signaling, screening, and selection. *Social Problems, 59*(3), 301–321.

Densley, J. A. (2014). It's gang life, but not as we know it: The evolution of gang business. *Crime and Delinquency, 60*(4), 517–546.

Densley, J. A., & Pyrooz, D. C. (2020). The matrix in context: Taking stock of police gang databases in London and beyond. *Youth Justice, 20*(1–2), 11–30.

Hesketh, R. F. (2019). Joining gangs: Living on the edge? *Journal of Criminological Research, Policy and Practice,* 280–294.

Hesketh, R. F., & Robinson, G. (2019). Grafting: "The boyz" just doing business? Deviant entrepreneurship in street gangs. *Safer Communities,* 54–63.

HM Government. (2011). Ending gang violence and youth violence: Cross government report, Home Office.

HM Government. (2020). Guidance for Criminal exploitation of children and vulnerable adults: County lines, Home Office.

Holligan, C., McLean, R., & McHugh, R. (2020). Exploring County lines: Criminal drug distribution practices in Scotland. *Youth Justice, 20*(1–2), 50–63.

McLean, R. (2018). An evolving gang model in contemporary Scotland. *Deviant Behavior, 39*(3), 309–321.

Melde, C., Diem, C., & Drake, G. (2012). Identifying correlates of stable gang membership. *Journal of Contemporary Criminal Justice, 28*(4), 482–498.

Moyle, L. (2019). Situating vulnerability and exploitation in street-level drug markets: Cuckooing, commuting, and the "County lines" drug supply model. *Journal of Drug Issues, 49*(4), 739–755.

Pyrooz, D. C., Sweeten, G., & Piquero, A. R. (2013). Continuity and change in gang membership and gang embeddedness. *Journal of Research in Crime and Delinquency, 50*(2), 239–271.

Sanchez, R. V., Speck, P. M., & Patrician, P. A. (2019). A concept analysis of trauma coercive bonding in the commercial sexual exploitation of children. *Journal of Pediatric Nursing, 46,* 48–54.

Sturrock, R., & Holmes, L. (2015). Running the risks: The links between gang involvement and young people going missing. *Catch 22.*

Warr, M. (2002). *Companions in crime: The social aspects of criminal conduct.* Cambridge University Press.

Whittaker, A., Densley, J., Cheston, L., Tyrell, T., Higgins, M., Felix-Baptiste, C., & Havard, T. (2020). Reluctant gangsters revisited: The evolution of gangs from postcodes to profits. *European Journal on Criminal Policy and Research*, *26*(1), 1–22.

Wood, J., & Alleyne, E. (2010). Street gang theory and research: Where are we now and where do we go from here? *Aggression and Violent Behavior*, *15*(2), 100–111.

Conclusion

This book has demonstrated how three independent sources of data can contribute to our understanding of risk and behavioral responses for young people who commit violent offenses. The **introduction** highlighted the importance of identifying behavioral patterns that are a common response to traumatic experiences, psychological, environmental, and social risks. **Chapter 1** demonstrated the need to differentiate between categories of offending according to motivation, role, and escalation. Applying a criminal narrative experience to young people who commit offenses permits further insight into why they offend and is particularly important for differentiating the roles of co-offenders. Distinguishing between expressive and instrumental violence is key to understanding how to prevent young people becoming justice involved, and the arrest data clearly demonstrate the different stages of instrumental and expressive behaviors (Figure 1.3).

    Chapter 2 differentiated between the stages and motivations for drug use, from social use of cannabis to experimentation with secondary drugs, ending in "self-medication" as a response to trauma (Figure 2.1). It also highlighted how drug selling to fund a social habit can increase a young person's vulnerability to exploitation and involvement with street-level gangs and organized crime. **Chapter 3** explored expressive violence as an early behavioral indicator of increased risk of family trauma, adverse childhood experiences, mental illness, and an inability to control impulsivity. This last factor can also be related to neurodiverse children and young people with conditions such as ADHD. The offenses of assault, domestic violence, criminal damage, and fighting represented the first stage of a potential pathway to involvement in serious violence and criminal syndicates.

    Chapter 4 differentiated between categories of knife crime and identified four stages of knife carrying and use (Figure 4.1), namely, external sources (fear or social pressure, including being coerced to carry a knife for someone else); carrying as part of self or group identity; habitual carrying and reactive use; and carrying with the intent to use a weapon for

DOI: 10.4324/9781003255697-9

instrumental purposes. **Chapter 5** explored sensation-seeking behaviors that typically occur in the presence of others. Examples of criminal damage because of a thrill-seeking activity, arson, breaking into a building or site, vehicle theft, joyriding, and hate crimes were discussed. The role of early sensation seeking in the later development of instrumental violence is also highlighted. Similarly, **Chapter 6** considered the relationship of nonviolent income-generating offenses such as shoplifting and theft to more serious acquisitive offending. It highlighted the importance of handling stolen items, domestic burglary, and theft of a motor vehicle as early indicators of criminal exploitation. It also highlighted the relationship of robbery to group offending and other instrumental violent behaviors.

Chapter 7 showed that young people who have been criminally exploited by adult gangs and organized crime do not necessarily see their involvement in the same way. This chapter stressed the need to understand how young people who have experienced exploitation see of their experiences. The chapter also differentiated between types of criminal groups and the processes of exploitation. Excerpts from interviews with young people who self-reported involvement with serious and organized crime illustrate their experiences in their own words. Based on data from all three studies, the chapter includes a model showing the process of exploitation, through known associates and strangers (Figure 7.1).

Overall, the contents of this book outline the complex relationship of psychological, social, and behavioral factors to expressive and instrumental violence. The outcome is dependent upon how young people navigate criminal networks among families, peers, and adult criminals with the sole intention of exploitation. It is also contingent upon how they negotiate an illegal sub-economy that can offer status, excitement, and financial rewards to participants who otherwise feel that they would not have these opportunities. This in turn provides a supply of criminally experienced, yet vulnerable, young people to serve those involved with organized crime, county lines drug dealing, and child exploitation.

The book sets out a common (but preventable) trajectory from expressive and reactive violence to thrill-seeking and income-generating offending. If unsupported, young people can be identified by older criminals who can expose them to heightened levels of violence and personal risk. There are opportunities to intervene from the first time that a young person offends. A key element of this approach is that while recognizing the commonality of activities on this path, each young person has individual personal factors of a highly dynamic nature that need to be identified and addressed. It is essential for this purpose to look at all behaviors comprehensively and to provide support for all vulnerabilities.

Young people commit the same offenses for different reasons and obtain person-specific rewards that are often unapparent from official records and assessments. Understanding how a young person experiences offending and how they view their role in the orchestration of an offense offers a valuable insight to identifying alternative behaviors and responses to criminal opportunities. A comprehensive multisystemic approach to supporting adolescents is required. This must include the family setting and the educational environment, and, where appropriate, the wider social networks need to be accounted for.

Arrest data offer a glimpse into the relationship between crime and the individual, but it is crucial to enable a young person to share their own experiences with practitioners who support them. One of the young people from Study C said that he did not feel he could share his experiences of violence as part of an organized criminal group with those who supported him. This was partly due to the fear of repercussions and incrimination, but also because he had been so disturbed by what he had witnessed and been a part of. These layers of trauma can be generational within families and are exacerbated by exposure to adult criminal activities and exploitation. Many young people who had reached this stage masked their experiences by using illegal substances, thus increasing their risk, and decreasing the likelihood of supported desistance.

Index

Page numbers in **bold** mark the locations of tables, while page numbers in *italics* represent figures.